ART & REALITY

ART & REALITY

THE NEW STANDARD

REFERENCE GUIDE AND
BUSINESS PLAN
FOR ACTIVELY DEVELOPING
YOUR CAREER AS AN ARTIST

by Robert J. Abbott

SEVEN LOCKS PRESS
Santa Ana, California
Minneapolis, Minnesota
Washington, D.C.

Library of Congress Cataloging-in-Publication Data

Abbott, Robert J., 1945–
Art & Reality: The New Standard Reference Guide and Business Plan for Actively Developing Your Career As an Artist / by Robert J. Abbott
p. cm.
Includes index.
ISBN 0-929765-56-7
1. Art--United States--Marketing I. Title.

PN8600.A19 1997
706'.8'8--dc21 97-10640
CIP

SECOND EDITION

Seven Locks Press
P.O. Box 25689
Santa Ana, CA 92799
(800) 354-5348

Contents

PREFACE

If you are happy with your artwork but frustrated by lack of success with the business side of the art world, then it is time to change your strategy. This book was conceived to meet the needs of the artist who wants to have a successful career. The information in this book will be valuable not only to the established artist but also to the entry level artist.

A wide chasm exists between artists and galleries, museums, and other exhibition spaces. This gap has been created by the inability of artists to present their works effectively to venues that can help advance their careers. This book was created to help artists and to help them reach the highest level of success they are capable of attaining in the shortest period of time.

In planning your career as an artist, it is imperative to know where you have been, where you are now, and where you want to go. If you are to attain success, you must understand the workings of the art world—the rules by which you play the game.

Once you know the who, what, when, where, why, and especially how to get your work shown, you can plan a strategy and build your career. Having knowledge and focus will eliminate speculation, confusion, and costly mistakes. Information not shared by the art world is offered to you with money-saving tips and techniques for success. You will develop the knowledge to recognize and take advantage of opportunities that present themselves to you.

The methods presented in this book are the result of years of firsthand experience in bringing an artist's work out of the studio and into the public arena. As director of the Modern Museum of Art in Southern California, I was bombarded by artists seeking to exhibit their work and find representation. Successful interaction between a director, curator, or dealer and an artist often comes down to the effectiveness of the artist's presentation. Although I have seen hundreds of presentations, the majority were at best mediocre. I began to see clearly what made the difference between success and failure. This book was created to set the standard of presentation by which the art world measures an artist's work.

Robert J. Abbott

HOW TO USE THIS BOOK

Art & Reality guides you step-by-step through the process of developing and executing a fast track career plan.

The best way to use this book is to start with Chapter 1, "Analysis—Artist Evaluation Survey." The evaluation will give you the opportunity to get your bearings and determine your current position. Armed with this knowledge, you can progress quickly through the book and start advancing your career. An appendix of suggested readings on each of the various topics discussed in this book has been provided for your reference. Many of these resources are available at your local or university libraries.

This book is designed to be worked in and referred to throughout your career. Many chapters include worksheets. Samples have been completed in this book to show you what information to look for or action to take. Blank copies of the worksheets are provided in the back of the book for copying and future use.

This book is also designed to lay flat for handsfree use and easy worksheet copying.

ABOUT THE AUTHOR

Author and noted lecturer Robert Abbott believes education and planning are the keys to success for any artist. "You must understand the needs of the people you are approaching, how to present your work, and how your art can succeed within their venue. There are many diverse markets within the art community open to the knowledgeable artist. A successful career is attainable if you plan and persevere."

As director of the Modern Museum of Art in Southern California, Abbott was responsible for bringing an extended series of major exhibitions to the area. He also was instrumental in the development of the nation's most exemplary arts educational outreach program, "Communication in the Arts," as recognized by the U.S. Department of Education. In *Art & Reality* he breaks down the seemingly impenetrable world of art, with all its complexities, idiosyncrasies, and politics, and offers artists all the tools needed to be successful in the business of art.

As president of the fine art publishing firm Fine Art Communication Technologies Inc., he developed the publishing careers of numerous artists. As he has commented, "There are many ways to publish your work, even on a modest budget. Once again, the key is educating yourself to your options and what will work for you."

This edition of *Art & Reality* is Abbott's newest contribution to the art world. According to the author, "*Art & Reality* is not merely a how-to book, but a career guide for the artist who wants to succeed quickly. Whether you are well seasoned or just starting out, *Art & Reality* is a must for those serious about a future in art."

1 ANALYSIS—ARTIST EVALUATION SURVEY

The first step in developing a successful career plan is to clearly understand where you are in your career now.

The survey on the following pages asks you to evaluate your present work. Reflect on your activities to date and the results they have produced. Assess the quality of your education and whether it has helped you or how a lack of recent educational pursuits has possibly hindered you. List the venues where your art has been shown. Finally, decide what you want your future to be. These responses will be the foundation on which you will build your career plan.

1. Complete the Analysis Thoroughly and Honestly

Be *honest* with yourself. Set aside an hour or two to think about the questions being posed. Answer each question completely. Rambling, tangential answers will only serve to confuse you later in the process.

2. Review Your Answers

After you have completed the analysis, reread your answers critically. If you find you are uncertain about some, you may have discovered a topic that requires further thought on your part.

3. Make a Decision About Your Direction

Make a decision in the direction you wish to proceed. Together we will examine your choices, what they mean, and how they can be used to ultimately build *your* career plan. With action by you, your plan can achieve results.

4. Never Be Discouraged

When you have completed the self-evaluation, you will probably feel like you have undergone microscopic scrutiny and you may be somewhat discouraged. Don't be. Rather, be encouraged that you are now taking control of your future.

EXAMPLE: ARTIST EVALUATION SURVEY

Date *12/10/97*

Artist Name *Michelle Talvison*

Address *1556 South Watkins Drive, Los Angeles, CA 90046*

Telephone *(213) 555-1212*

Facsimile *(213) 555-2323*

E-Mail ____________

Internet ____________

Art

1. Describe your work.

   Abstract figurative—much of my work deals with social issues. Over the last three years my work has developed a strong continuity, both in my paintings and sculpture pieces.

2. Describe the style of your work.

   Again, I would say my works would probably be called abstract expressionism by most people—although I have my own unique style. Some people compare my work to that of Edward Munch and Keifer. I tend to use the human figure in much of my work, which seems to make it more accessible than pure abstraction.

3. How long have you worked in this style?

   I began working in this style about five years ago, but it really began to come together three years ago. My style has not changed a lot since that time, only matured in the same technique.

4. Has your style changed? Yes ____ No *x*

5. Do you change your style frequently? Infrequently? Describe.

   Not often over the past three years. Early in my career, I experimented on a regular basis. I seem to have found a style that works for me.

6. Describe the materials, media, and general dimensions of your art.

   I like to work with large canvases—anywhere from 48" square to 6' x 8'. I use oil and acrylic and often work with bronzes made from plasters. I use dark colors, often bleeding them for unusual imagery.

7. Briefly, what is your artistic philosophy?

   To express my ideas in a gestural way—to allow the viewer a glimpse into my ideas. I do this with imagery and color.

8. Where do you get your inspiration for works?

   From everything around me—my daily experiences in life—particularly tensions in the world, the beauty of nature, and people's inability to deal with one another.

9. Do you feel you have a good understanding of your philosophy?

   Yes __*x*__ No _____ Why?

   I try to understand my subject matter to its fullest before I try to express my philosophy on canvas or in bronze. I do a lot of reading and a lot of studying. My goal is to alert others to the effects the subject matter has on their daily lives.

10. Do you feel others understand your philosophy?

    Yes *x* No ____ Why?

    I have shown my work in exhibitions and had the opportunity to talk to those attending. For the most part they see my message. They may not agree with it, but they understand what I am saying.

11. What other artists do you admire?

    Jasper Johns, Pablo Picasso, Andy Warhol, Georgia O'Keeffe, and many more.

12. What inspires you about their work?

    I like the freedom they seem to have had in producing work—that they did what they wanted to do rather than being dictated to or controlled by other influences. I admire artists such as Andy Warhol who have explored new boundaries or ideas.

13. Compare your art to other artists' in terms of style, quality, technique, and price.

    I would say that my work is something like that of Jasper Johns and Andy Warhol—a combination of both. My technique has become pretty strong as I have been developing it now for six years. The quality is good—some pieces are stronger than others. My prices are not at all where I wish they were, although in the area where I live, they are above average.

14. Write a one-paragraph biography of yourself as an artist.

    Born: New York City, 1959. I studied at New York University, graduating with an M.F.A. in 1984. After graduation, I worked as a studio assistant for Anthony Michaels. Under his tutelage, I experimented with styles, media, and expression of ideas. Two years later I began exhibiting a consistent body of works and lecturing to university students about my media techniques. In the process of continuing my education, I have made contacts with educators from across the country, and some have helped me obtain exhibitions.

Market Survey

Understanding the possible marketplaces for your work is an important aspect of developing a successful career plan. Avenues through which you have had prior achievements may only be the tip of the iceberg. With good planning and an open mind, you will discover other possible venues for your work.

15. Where do you feel your work best fits?

Galleries ___*x*___

Museums ___*x*___

Art Fairs ______

Retail Stores ______

Other(s) *Colleges and universities*

16. Does your art have a geographical influence, i.e., seascapes, etc.?

Not really—I would say it is universal in content and subject matter.

17. In what geographical areas do most of the people who collect your art live?

Primarily the East Coast and metropolitan areas. I have a few collectors from Europe.

18. Does your art appeal to the general public or to a more "art educated" sector? Please elaborate.

The art educated sector. My work is quite colorful, but the subject matter is "tough." I seem to sell to people who collect more than decorate.

19. What types of galleries have shown your work?

In the area where I live, I show in the best galleries with recognized on the edge artists. These galleries show fine art of contemporary artists: paintings, sculptures, and graphic pieces.

20. What types of museums have shown your work?

    I have shown my work in two group museum shows. Although the museums focus on contemporary European artists, they hold yearly shows for local artists.

21. What types of other places have shown your work?

    I have had good results at colleges and universities. Shows in libraries, banks, art fairs, and similar places have been difficult because of the aggressive subject matter of my work.

22. What price range has your art sold in?

    Through galleries *$600 - $2,200*

    Through your studio *$100 - $2,200*

    Through art fairs ______

    Through other venues ______

23. Has your art ever been published? (i.e., limited edition prints, etc.)

    Self-Published _____ Publishing Company _____ Never Published *x*

24. What price range were the published works sold for? *N/A*

25. How many pieces were published in each edition? *N/A*

26. What method of printing was used to publish your work?

    N/A

27. Were you satisfied with the results? Explain your answer.

    N/A

28. If you have not been published, would you be interested in publishing your work? Explain your answer.

    Yes *x* No _____

    People frequently ask me if I have something in print. I feel I could offer something in a price range that is affordable to more people yet keep the integrity of what I have achieved to date.

Shows and Exhibitions

List any and all shows and exhibitions in which you have participated to date. Include information on location, dates, group or solo, works on display, coordinator of the event, and the like. If you have a current biography sheet, simply attach it to this section. If you are a new artist or have not shown your works extensively, do not be discouraged. You have wisely chosen to carefully plan your introduction to the art world.

29. Galleries/Commercial Spaces

(I am only listing the last three years.)

1995, Time-Space Gallery, New York, NY. Group show.

1995, Coll Gallery, Chicago, IL. Group show.

1995, Roskins Gallery, Los Angeles, CA. Solo exhibition.

1995, Daniel James Gallery, San Jose, CA. Group show.

1995, Time-Space Gallery, New York, NY. Group show.

1996, Coll Gallery, Chicago, IL. Solo exhibition.

1997, LA Contemporary Arts, Los Angeles, CA. Group show.

30. Museums/Institutions

1997, Mockteller Museum, San Francisco, CA. Group show.

1997, Alternative Museum, Los Angeles, CA. Group show.

31. Alternative Spaces

1997, New Arts Alternative Space, Chicago, IL. Group show.

1997, The Temporary Contemporary, Chicago, IL. Group show.

32. School Exhibitions

1995, Fine Arts Gallery, Lexington Art School, Lexington, KY. Group show.

1996, Alumni Exhibition, New York University, New York, NY. Group show.

1997, Alumni Exhibition, New York University, New York, NY. Group show.

33. Competitions

1997 Tri-State Arts Festival, Sacramento, CA - 2nd place - sculpture

1997 New England Fine Arts Council Competition, Boston, MA - 1st place - sculpture

34. Public Spaces

N/A

35. Private Collections

Dr. & Mrs. Richard Elliott, Boston, MA

Mockteller Museum Collection, San Francisco, CA

Alternative Museum Collection, Los Angeles, CA

Thomas Coll Collection, Chicago, IL

New York University Alumni Collection, New York, NY

36. Art Fairs/Festivals

1996 Los Angeles Art Fair, Los Angeles, CA

1996 Miami Art Celebration, Miami, FL

37. Other(s)

N/A

38. Are you an active member of an arts organization? A museum? Describe.

Yes. I am a member of the Mockteller Museum Volunteer Guild. Each year I help organize the fund-raising auction and the children's exhibition.

39. Are you involved in any community work relating to the arts? Describe.

Yes. I volunteer my services twice a month to a local mental health institution for resident artworkshops. The patients' art has an uninhibited self-expression that helps their treatment and my personal growth as an artist.

Education

Education can be an important facet in the development of your career as a professional artist. It helps you be aware of the evolution of art throughout the history of humankind, of art's influence on social values and perceptions of the times, and of the power that individual artists have had on society. Education, either formal or informal, broadens you as an artist and contributes to your understanding of the realms and responsibilities of an artist. Although formal education is not a requirement for becoming an artist, keeping informed will help expand your opportunities.

40. What art education have your received? Include the dates and locations of high school, college, and continuing education as appropriate.

    1981–84, M.F.A. - New York University, New York, NY

    1977–81, B.A. - California Arts College, Sacramento, CA

    1973–77, Sacramento High School, Sacramento, CA

41. Have you studied art history or other art-related courses? Please elaborate.

    Yes. Two years of art history studies during M.F.A. work. I explored the many periods of art and their influences upon and by society.

42. Have you interned with another artist or institution? Attended artist workshops?

    I was a studio assistant for Anthony Michaels. I try to attend workshops and lectures of artists I respect.

43. Do you visit the shows and exhibitions of other artists on a fairly regular basis?

    Yes __*x*__ No _____

44. What types of education are you involved in at this time or planning to be involved in in the near future?

    I attend workshops and lectures regularly. I am interested in applying for an artist-in-residency program abroad. (Italy or France is my preference.)

Goals

45. What are your short-term (six month) goals for your art career?

    1. To organize my work into a cohesive presentation.

    2. To obtain my first actual dealer/representative.

    3. To apply for an artist-in-residency program.

    4. To publish a small limited edition of two pieces of my work.

46. What are your two-year goals?

    1. To firmly establish myself in Southern California.

    2. To begin establishing myself in New York, aiming for Europe.

    3. To apply and receive an artist-in-residency grant in Europe.

47. What are your five-year goals?

    1. To sell and show my works throughout the United States and Europe.

    2. To exhibit in a number of European museums.

    3. To have more museum shows in general.

48. What would be your ultimate achievement—the goal of all goals—for you as an artist?

    To create work that is considered historically important by my peers and the art community.

49. Is selling your work a major factor in your art career?

    Yes __*x*__ No _____ Why?

    I have chosen art as my lifelong career. I need to sell works to purchase more supplies to create more work. Teaching helps to supplement my income and keeps me in touch with the art community.

50. Are you willing and able to financially support the expenses of developing your career, such as presentation materials, travel, and other activities?

    Yes __*x*__ No _____

Productivity

51. How much time do you devote to your work?

    In a day? *3 - 4 hours*

    In a week? *18 - 25 hours*

52. How long, on an average, does it take to complete a piece?

    Depending upon the complexity of the piece, anywhere from one hour to three days.

53. What percentage of your work product would you consider strong enough for exhibition in your chosen market?

    Approximately 75 percent. I only keep those pieces that I feel are strong.

54. How prolific are you? How many pieces do you complete?

    In a week? *1 - 2 paintings and 5 drawings*

    In a month? *3 - 6 paintings*

    In a year? *A lot if need be.*

55. Are you able to support yourself through the sales of your works?

    Yes __x__ No _____

56. Are you employed at another job?

    Full time _____ Part time __x__ None _____

57. How many times a year do you present your work?

    To galleries? *3*

    To museums? *0*

58. Do you call on galleries where you do not know anyone ("cold call")?

    Yes _____ No __x__

59. Do you call on museums where you do not know anyone ("cold call")?

    Yes _____ No __x__

60. How many quality pieces do you presently have available for exhibition? *10*

61. How do you handle rejection?

    Fairly well. I frequently solicit opinions of my work from people I respect.

YOUR ARTIST EVALUATION SURVEY

The following pages contain a blank survey for you to complete. Although it does require a modest investment of time and thought, it provides valuable information for developing your career plan. Retain your completed evaluation for future reference.

Before the Survey

A few of the artists who have used this book at first were reluctant to complete the survey. After completing it, however, they all said they had a better understanding of what they hoped to achieve and that the survey helped define who they were as artists.

I've had artists at all levels, including some of the most successful in the United States, purchase this book. All have been able to use the information for their specific needs. One renowned artist, although doing very well financially, felt he wasn't receiving the recognition from the art community he thought he deserved. After reviewing his evaluation and presentation materials, I was able to suggest a different presentation. This new presentation was much more suitable for the venues he was targeting. Subsequently, the presentation opened up new opportunities for him.

No matter where you are in your career, once you commit your goals to paper you will begin to focus your efforts and define a path to your future success.

ARTIST EVALUATION SURVEY

Date ______________________________

Artist Name ______________________________

Address ______________________________

Telephone ______________________________

Facsimile ______________________________

E-Mail ______________________________

Internet ______________________________

Art

1. Describe your work.

____

____

____

____

2. Describe the style of your work.

____

____

____

____

3. How long have you worked in this style?

____

____

____

____

4. Has your style changed? Yes _____ No _____

5. Do you change your style frequently? Infrequently? Describe.

____

____

____

____

6. Describe the materials, media, and general dimensions of your art.

____

____

____

____

7. Briefly, what is your artistic philosophy?

____

____

____

____

8. Where do you get your inspiration for works?

____

____

____

____

9. Do you feel you have a good understanding of your philosophy?

   Yes _____ No _____ Why?

____

____

____

____

10. Do you feel others understand your philosophy?

    Yes _____ No _____ Why?

    ____

    ____

    ____

    ____

11. What other artists do you admire?

    ____

    ____

    ____

12. What inspires you about their work?

    ____

    ____

    ____

    ____

13. Compare your art to other artists' in terms of style, quality, technique, and price.

    ____

    ____

    ____

    ____

14. Write a one-paragraph biography of yourself as an artist.

    ____

    ____

    ____

    ____

    ____

    ____

    ____

Market Survey

Understanding the possible marketplaces for your work is an important aspect of developing a successful career plan. Avenues through which you have had prior achievements may only be the tip of the iceberg. With good planning and an open mind, you will discover other possible venues for your work.

15. Where do you feel your work best fits?

    Galleries _____

    Museums _____

    Art Fairs _____

    Retail Stores _____

    Other(s) ______________________________

16. Does your art have a geographical influence, i.e., seascapes, etc.?

    ____

    ____

    ____

17. In what geographical areas do most of the people who collect your art live?

    ____

    ____

    ____

18. Does your art appeal to the general public or to a more "art educated" sector? Please elaborate.

    ____

    ____

    ____

19. What types of galleries have shown your work?

    ____

    ____

    ____

20. What types of museums have shown your work?

____

____

21. What types of other places have shown your work?

____

____

22. What price range has your art sold in?

Through galleries ____________________

Through your studio ____________________

Through art fairs ____________________

Through other venues ____________________

23. Has your art ever been published? (i.e., limited edition prints, etc.)

Self-published _____ Publishing Company _____ Never Published _____

24. What price range were the published works sold for? __________

25. How many pieces were published in each edition? __________

26. What method of printing was used to publish your work?

____

____

27. Were you satisfied with the results? Explain your answer.

____

____

____

28. If you have not been published, would you be interested in publishing your work? Explain your answer.

Yes _____ No _____

____

____

____

Shows and Exhibitions

List any and all shows and exhibitions in which you have participated to date. Include information on location, dates, group or solo, works on display, coordinator of the event, and the like. If you have a current biography sheet, simply attach it to this section. If you are a new artist or have not shown your works extensively, do not be discouraged. You have wisely chosen to carefully plan your introduction to the art world.

29. Galleries/Commercial Spaces

____

____

____

____

____

____

____

____

30. Museums/Institutions

____

____

____

31. Alternative Spaces

____

____

____

32. School Exhibitions

____

____

____

33. Competitions

34. Public Spaces

35. Private Collections

36. Art Fairs/Festivals

37. Other(s)

38. Are you an active member of an arts organization? A museum? Describe.

39. Are you involved in any community work relating to the arts? Describe.

Education

Education can be an important facet in the development of your career as a professional artist. It helps you be aware of the evolution of art throughout the history of humankind, of art's influence on social values and perceptions of the times, and of the power that individual artists have had on society. Education, either formal or informal, broadens you as an artist and contributes to your understanding of the realms and responsibilities of an artist. Although formal education is not a requirement for becoming an artist, keeping informed will help expand your opportunities.

40. What art education have your received? Include the dates and locations of high school, college, and continuing education as appropriate.

____

____

____

41. Have you studied art history or other art-related courses? Please elaborate.

____

____

42. Have you interned with another artist or institution? Attended artist workshops?

____

____

43. Do you visit the shows and exhibitions of other artists on a fairly regular basis?

    Yes _____ No _____

44. What types of education are you involved in at this time or planning to be involved in in the near future?

____

____

Goals

45. What are your short-term (six month) goals for your art career?

____

____

____

____

46. What are your two-year goals?

____

____

____

47. What are your five-year goals?

____

____

____

48. What would be your ultimate achievement—the goal of all goals—for you as an artist?

____

____

49. Is selling your work a major factor in your art career?

Yes _____ No _____ Why?

____

____

____

50. Are you willing and able to financially support the expenses of developing your career, such as presentation materials, travel, and other activities?

Yes _____ No _____

Productivity

51. How much time do you devote to your work?

In a day? _______________

In a week? _______________

52. How long, on an average, does it take to complete a piece?

____

53. What percentage of your work product would you consider strong enough for exhibition in your chosen market?

____

54. How prolific are you? How many pieces do you complete?

    In a week? ____________________

    In a month? ____________________

    In a year? ____________________

55. Are you able to support yourself through the sales of your works?

    Yes _____ No _____

56. Are you employed at another job?

    Full Time _____ Part Time _____ None _____

57. How many times a year do you present your work?

    To galleries? ____

    To museums? ____

58. Do you call on galleries where you do not know anyone ("cold call")?

    Yes _____ No _____

59. Do you call on museums where you do not know anyone ("cold call")?

    Yes _____ No _____

60. How many quality pieces do you presently have available for exhibition? _____

61. How do you handle rejection?

    ____

    ____

    ____

    ____

    ____

EVALUATING YOUR SURVEY

Now that you have completed the survey, it is time for you to evaluate your answers and learn where you are and where you want to go. Start the evaluation by reviewing your answers and then respond to the questions below. After you have completed your evaluation, a direction will be defined for you. And when you move in that direction, you will be on your way to success.

(Check the answers that apply to you.)

Questions 1–6

Develop a description of your work. If you change your work continually and don't have a focus, you need to establish a direction. Do not show work that is all over the board. It is important to have a cohesive body of work—or to be building one—to present.

Do you feel you have a good understanding of your work and your style and does your work have a definite focus?

Yes _____ No _____ Not Sure _____

Questions 7–10

If you have a philosophy, it's important that you communicate it to the viewer and continue expanding upon your philosophy. If you don't have any particular philosophy, that's fine. What is important is that you know who you are as an artist and have a specific focus.

Do you understand what inspires you to produce work and do you have a philosophical communication with your viewers?

Yes _____ No _____ Not Sure _____

Questions 11–14

Have you studied the works of other artists—historic or contemporary? Do you feel you have a knowledge of art, art movements, and art history?

Yes _____ No _____ Not Sure _____

If you answered no, you may wish to explore this area. Such study can help to expand your artistic possibilities.

Questions 15–18

Whether you have collectors or not, are you addressing questions that need to be answered in order to plan your career? If you are not sure, you may seek the opinion of someone you respect.

Do you feel you have a relatively good understanding of these questions?

Yes _____ No _____ Not Sure _____

Questions 19–21

These questions asked about venues where you have shown your work. If you've exhibited in academic venues but wish to pursue a more commercial direction or if you are a commercially-oriented artist, you need to draw the line and focus on those venues that are in your chosen area.

Can you make a decision on the direction to pursue representation in the future?

Yes _____ No _____ Not Sure _____

Question 22

Establish prices for your work that are comparable to those of artists of similar stature. Keep in mind it is important to maintain current knowledge of market prices.

Do you feel you have a good idea what your work should sell for?

Yes _____ No _____ Not Sure _____

Questions 23–28

In developing a publishing business the key is to thoroughly understand the market you wish to enter. Do not be misled by printers who claim you will make a fortune. Keep in mind printers are interested in selling printing, not prints.

If you answered yes to Question 28, read thoroughly "Publishing Your Work," on pages 141–150.

Questions 29–39

This part of the survey encouraged you to keep in mind the many venues where you can present work on a continual basis. Frequent exposure increases the likelihood that you will receive representation. When possible, try to involve yourself in local art-related functions.

Do you feel you are ready and have the knowledge to approach possible venues with your work?

Yes _____ No _____ Not Sure _____

Questions 40–44

Education is important. It need not be formal or institutional learning, but if you wish to advance your career financially, intellectually, and emotionally, you must be knowledgeable and current.

Are you willing to invest time seeking information that can further your career?

Yes _____ No _____ Not Sure _____

Questions 45–50

Your goals are most important because they enable you to plan a course of action to reach your objectives. Set short- and long-term goals, but be realistic. If you pursue your goals in a planned fashion, you will likely succeed. You may have to adjust your goals along the way, but that's part of the trip. Always pursue and be persistent.

Like any business venture, art requires expense. After all, if you start a new business, you have to buy some equipment. If you are careful and conservative, the cost will not be excessive. I tell artists to think of art as a business because it is.

Are you willing to purchase the necessary materials and pay for other expenses necessary to begin a career as an artist? Keep in mind that costs can vary widely.

Yes _____ No _____ Not Sure _____

Questions 51–56

It is important to produce enough work to show to venues. If your output is limited to a few works a year, you may not be able to support yourself with your art. Even so, you can still show your work. Many artists I work with are more interested in institutional exhibitions than in sales. What is important is that you are producing and continuing to develop and present your work.

Are you producing a cohesive body of work in sufficient quantity for exhibition or presentation?

Yes _____ No _____ Not Sure _____

Questions 57–60

From the many evaluations I've done with both experienced, full-time artists and newcomers, I'm amazed to discover most of them present their works only a few times a year. In business you don't stop building your business after you make the first sale. You continue to build.

Are you willing to present your work on a continual basis until you succeed?

Yes _____ No _____ Not Sure _____

Question 61

If you can't handle rejection, you're in the wrong business. A fine artist, just like artists in music, drama, theater, or film, will encounter many obstacles along the way. But the rewards are great for those who persevere. One artist responded to how he handled rejection: "Just another opportunity to present my work."

Can you handle rejection?

Yes _____ No _____ Not Sure _____

Note: If you answered "no" or "not sure" to five or more of the survey evaluation questions, then you need to refocus your direction.

FACT PRODUCTS AND SERVICES

After you have completed your evaluation, you may feel you need professional assistance to get your career on the right track. Fine Arts Communications Technologies, Inc. (FACT) can help.

FACT is a full-service company that was founded to meet the needs of professional artists. FACT offers a number of services and products, including *Art & Reality*, a complete book and reference guide for developing a career in the arts.

Fees upon Request

Contact FACT at the phone number, address, or Internet site listed on page 27.

Professional Evaluation and Career Consultation

After you have completed your evaluation, if you feel you need professional assistance to get your career on the right track, you may arrange for a consultation. Send your evaluation along with slides or photographs of your work to the address listed. If you live close to the FACT offices, you may schedule an appointment.

Representation

FACT offers a service of representing artists' work to galleries, museums, universities, publishers, architects, designers, art consultants, and exhibition organizers.

Printing and Publishing

FACT specializes in printing and publishing services for artists. FACT offers full color as well as black and white and other printed materials at affordable prices. Catalog design, layout, essay writing, and complete promotional packaging are also available.

FACT Reference Library

Artists, galleries, museums, and other institutions using FACT's printing or publishing services are automatically included in the FACT reference library. The library is used by other galleries, institutions, designers, and art consultants wishing to purchase or exhibit art.

Art & Reality Book

Art & Reality is the new complete book and reference guide for developing a career in the arts.

Art & Reality Audio Tape

This motivational audio tape, available in 1997, will assist artists in starting and expanding their art careers.

FINE ART COMMUNICATION TECHNOLOGIES, INC.
30812 Pacific Coast Highway
Laguna Beach, CA 92677
Tel: (714)499-8300 Fax: (714)499-8311
E-Mail: artreality@aol.com
The Internet: http:/www.fineartcommtech.com

ANSWERS TO FREQUENTLY ASKED QUESTIONS

Artists often ask me questions. Here are my answers to the questions I am most often asked. Perhaps you have similar questions. The answers may provide you some direction.

Questions most often asked by entry-level artists:

Can I make money with my art?

If art similar to yours is selling, then yes. If your work is very different from anything on the market, then possibly. Research will be the key.

When would be a good time to present my art?

When you have a body of work together and are inspired.

How much should I sell my work for?

It depends on prior sales prices and what research shows similar works of art of the same quality and stature sell for.

How many works should I have before I go to a gallery?

A minimum of ten and a maximum of twenty visually cohesive pieces.

Is it worthwhile to enter competitions?

Yes, they can provide visibility and open up opportunities.

I don't want to sell my original paintings. Should I make prints?

If you wish to make money, it's the only way. But reconsider sales. As an artist you can always paint another painting. And work you don't want to part with now may not be as important to you in the future.

Where can I show my work?

Many places if you target your options. Be realistic. Make sure your materials are in order. And pursue every opportunity!

Can I work in a number of styles?

If you are going after galleries, you should probably stay with one style. If you are in the decorative arts, use whatever style it takes to make the sale.

Questions most often asked by established artists:

Where should I go to present my work?

Research is critical here. In what types of galleries have you been showing? What price range is your work? Select galleries that represent types of work similar in style and price to yours. Remember, those galleries handle what their collectors buy.

How can I get into publishing?

Select works that have sold or could have sold many times. Evaluate reproduction options: stone lithography, etchings, serigraphy, Iris, and offset lithography. Be conservative initially and willing to try alternatives in the future.

What can I do to increase my income?

Many things: increase your prices, your representation, and your production. Of most importance, however, increase your knowledge and pursuit of available markets and opportunities.

I want to upgrade the level of galleries in which I am currently represented. What should I do?

Have people whose opinions you trust suggest representation that they think would be a suitable vertical move. Make sure your presentation materials are in order. See Chapter 5, "Developing Your Presentation Materials."

How can I get my work into museums?

Present your work to them. If you have a catalog, ask the museums to include it in their reference library. Often it is easier to get your work into a group exhibition than a solo exhibition. I recommend that artists get involved at local museums. It can open up possibilities through contacts.

I have recently moved across the country. Whom should I approach?

Be selective. Identify the people and galleries you want to represent you and pursue opportunities with them one at a time. If you've done business with a gallery in your former hometown, ask for any contacts it might have in your new town.

2 PLANNING STRATEGIES/ BUILDING YOUR PLAN

QUICK TIP

Will my work fit with the other work in this gallery?

To reach your career objectives, you need a plan—one with the components that will ensure your success. The following sections summarize the steps necessary to develop and implement your career plan.

The Artist's Evaluation

By completing the evaluation survey, you've already taken the first step. The survey should have given you a clear understanding of where you have been in your career, where you are now, and where you want to be. For example, you should know whether you want to achieve financial success or historical importance, or a little of both.

The next steps are building your plan and gathering the materials and knowledge you will need to execute that plan successfully.

Developing a career is an ongoing and evolutionary process. At this time, you are just starting the process. As you carry out your plan and learn more about the world of art, you will make adjustments, research new opportunities, and update and create new materials.

Defining Your Art—Who Are You?

The goal in describing your art is to convince people to see it. Many artists do not put into writing what their art is about. You will need to describe your art, its media, style, and philosophy in a manner that moves people to view your work.

Exercise: Write an artist's statement.

Marketplaces and Opportunities

Before you begin marketing your art, you must understand what marketplaces are available. A well-thought-out career plan calls for marketing in more than one area.

Exercise: Select the primary and secondary marketplaces you wish to pursue.

Developing Your Presentation Materials

Unquestionably the most important step you take in your career will be to develop your presentation materials. Without them, you are out of business. You must continue to develop your work and knowledge and update your materials. These materials will often be the only liaison between yourself and a potential exhibition or sale. You have only one chance to make a first impression. Make it a success!

Exercises: Assemble your presentation materials.
Assemble your archive.

Catalog, Presentation Binder, and Brochure—Design and Development

The catalog is an important part of your presentation. Its purpose is to elevate the importance of your works and you as an artist. The catalog gives credibility and will distinguish you from the masses. Artworks and statements seen in print are taken far more seriously than those that are not.

Most artists recognize the need for a catalog but believe it is out of their financial reach. This is a misconception. By comparison-shopping the production and printing, you can develop a professional catalog of your works on a modest budget. Many galleries and museums are willing to share the expense of publishing a catalog. When you publish a catalog, it's important to use "perfect binding." (Most soft cover books are perfect bound.) This format allows a title to be printed on the catalog's spine, so it can be easily located on the shelves in museum and institutional catalog libraries.

If you think that your current budget will not let you create a catalog, consider a presentation binder or a brochure. A properly created binder can provide the visual impact needed to catch the attention of the viewer. The binder can also be easily updated with photographs of new works and copies of catalogs, brochures, and other print material.

A presentation brochure has the same elements as a catalog but in a condensed form, allowing you to produce an effective promotional piece on a smaller scale.

Exercises: Develop as complete a presentation package as funds allow:

1. Catalog
2. Presentation binder
3. Brochure

CD-ROM and Video Tape

New technology provides opportunities for artists who wish to remain on the cutting edge of promotional opportunities. CD-ROM and video tape catalogs and presentations are now cost effective for artists. The content for these electronic media should be is identical to the content I recommend for inclusion in a catalog.

One critical consideration in developing a CD-ROM or video tape catalog is the amount of art to be displayed. Don't overload your presentation. Limit an electronic catalog to ten or twenty examples of your work, with maximum continuity and a central focus. These formats can be a powerful presentation tools since they have the capacity to contain sound, video, text, and still photos. However, I strongly recommend that you do not limit yourself to a single form of presentation, especially when the medium is an emerging technology. Many academic venues and galleries still do not have the display hardware to take advantage of CD-ROMs and videotape so you should also be prepared with presentation binders, catalogs, or brochures.

The Internet is another fast emerging technology with attractive marketing possibilities for artists. You can get an incredible amount of exposure marketing on the World

Wide Web, but you still must do a significant amount of research to avoid some of the pitfalls of doing business in cyberspace. Numerous Internet consultants are available to answer questions and give advice, along with many publications available about how to establish a business presence on the Internet.

QUICK TIP

Is my work priced right for the gallery?

Again, don't limit yourself to a single format. Have a variety of materials available and use the right tool for the job.

Qualifying Your Targets

You may be a professional artist wishing to expand your exposure to more venues or you may be a part-time artist ready to try to get your work into a gallery. Either way, do not underestimate the value of doing your homework. Successful artists understand the importance of planning their actions. Aside from your talent and presentation materials, your knowledge about each venue you have targeted will put you on the right track, ultimately saving you time, money, and frustration.

Exercises: Develop an ongoing telephone research program.
Develop a record-keeping system for the information you gather.
Maintain a list of viable venues.

Presenting Your Work

At this point, you will begin to meet influential people within the art community. Tune up your interpersonal skills. Such skills are invaluable whenever you contact people to advance your career goals.

Exercises: Present your materials to the targeted venues.
Follow up with each presentation.
Develop a record-keeping system to document each contact, positive or negative, with the prospective venues.
Develop your mailing list.

Written Communications

It is important for you to be aware of how to write an effective business letter. A number of good books on the subject provide guidelines appropriate for business letters, or you can simply follow the letter formats in this book.

Exercises: Purchase stationery.
Develop your library of cover letters, follow-up letters, and thank-you notes.
Develop your résumé.

QUICK TIP

Always be professional.

Working with the Venues—Business and Legal Considerations

As an artist, you will have to sign contracts and agreements about your work. You need to be familiar with and thoroughly understand these documents.

Exercise: Develop your library of legal documents.

Promotions

Promotions can arouse the interest of collectors, galleries, art editors/writers, and other people who have influence in the art world. You may create this excitement through printed materials, print and electronic media, special events, and personal networking. In turn, their actions increase awareness of you and your work and add credibility to your position. The methods are not expensive but simply require ingenuity and perseverance on your part.

Exercises:
- Prepare for the promotional process.
- Develop promotions for your scheduled events.
- Develop long-term promotions for your overall career.
- Develop a promotions record-keeping process to stay attuned to what people are saying about your art.

Publishing Your Work

Publishing is often misunderstood. For the purpose of this book, we will define publishing as making multiple reproductions of a work. These reproductions are "limited editions" or a "series." Publishing is not limited to just the painter or photographer. Sculptors can also publish their work by creating a piece in bronze, for example, and then casting additional pieces.

Exercises:
- Evaluate the appropriateness of publishing within your career plan.
- Develop a publishing plan.
- Telephone research publishing companies.
- Explore self-publishing.
- Establish a method of distribution.
- Design and produce marketing materials for your published works.
- Publish your work.

Pricing Your Work

Pricing requires thorough research of the marketplaces you are targeting and the artists who are selling there. Remember to compare apples to apples. Look at successes of artists who are similar to you in style, medium, and importance. Don't inflate your expectations by asking a blue chip artist's sales prices, unless you are a blue-chip artist.

Exercises:
- Research the current market prices for artists of similar style, quality, and technique.
- Develop a wholesale/retail pricing structure for your present body of work.

Finding Funding for Your Work

As part of developing your career plan, consider the supportive opportunities made available to artists through grants, artist-in-residency programs, and sponsorships. Grants and programs for visual artists are available for all types of work and all types of artists. These programs can be used to obtain financial support and time to develop your work and career. Both you and the sponsoring organization benefit from these opportunities.

A grant is an award of cash or provision of materials based upon a given set of criteria. These criteria are determined by the sponsoring organization and are based upon the focus of the organization's efforts. An artist-in-residency program is a form of grant designed to provide artists with the opportunity to live and work in an environment conducive to artistic development. Sponsorships are projects funded by individuals, organizations, and corporations, again usually based upon the focus of the sponsor's activities or products.

Qualifications for a grant are established by the sponsoring organization and may include things such as birthplace, heritage, experience, age, sex, style of art, subject matter, project, religious affiliation, financial need, and similar factors. Grants are based upon just about any qualification you can think of and then some. It will be your job to search through the grant resources to find those that interest you. With an organized research effort, you may uncover opportunities for aid for which you are ideally qualified.

Exercise: Research funding resources (grants, residency programs, lecturing, benefactors.)

GETTING THERE FROM HERE

If you are an artist who has never tried to obtain representation, remember that you have nothing to lose and everything to gain. It is easy to achieve if you follow a realistic career plan. As you work through this book, you will gain confidence in yourself, your work, and your approach, and you will have a plan. Once you have your career plan, stick with it. The plan *will* work for you.

I often ask artists why they have not attempted to show their work. Many times they say they are not ready. Five years later they are still not ready. Fear of rejection holds them back. No matter how prepared you are and how good your art is, you are going to get rejections; you can't avoid them. Why some art has the public's approval and other art doesn't can't always be explained. Getting exhibitions will build your confidence, add to your biography, put rejection in perspective, and continue to advance your career.

Consistency

One of the biggest challenges you will face in marketing your art is making sure the pieces you choose to present are up-to-date, consistent with one another (as shown in the examples here), and convey your style and talent. Do not work under the assumption that by showing a variety of styles you are somehow demonstrating the scope of your skills. Such a pot-luck portfolio will only damage your potential for representation because few gallery directors are interested in trying to guess which of those styles is your real style. Unless your current work has strong ties with earlier work, avoid showing the two together. If you want to be taken seriously, you must produce a body of works that has strength and continuity and shows a well-defined sense of direction.

A prime example of this rule involves an artist I met while working at the museum. He had just returned from presenting his work in New York and was particularly discouraged by the response from one of the more prestigious galleries. The gallery director, a respected figure in the art community, had recommended that the artist "go home to California and take up a new profession." After looking at the work the artist had chosen to present, I could see the director's point. The portfolio contained what the artist felt was a good representation of his art, which might have worked for him had he been organizing a retrospective of everything he'd done since grammar school. Confronted with thirty years of the artist's best works demonstrating a major lack of consistency, the gallery director had every reason to be confused.

Almost as common as lack of continuity is the overabundance of it. If the art you are producing today bears an uncanny resemblance to work you were showing ten or twenty years ago, perhaps it is time for some adaptation. Several years ago, I asked a major collector about her most recent purchases and how she selected the works she purchased. "We collect what's happening now," was her response.

If you plan to be included in the sphere of marketable art, it is important to keep abreast of current trends in the art world. I am not suggesting that you change your style with every passing fad, nor would I recommend you copy the styles of the already established blue chip artists—their work falls into the category of "embalmed in art history." You can, however, expand your work without resorting to major surgery. Fine art and graphic art publications such as *ArtNews*, *Art in America*, and other magazines can keep you informed on the current interests of the major galleries and institutions. Once you have that information, it is simply a matter of experimenting and further developing your work. *Remember, if you believe in your work, others will too.*

3 DESCRIBING YOUR ART—WHO ARE YOU?

Describing Your Art and Yourself

QUICK TIP

Stay focused.

The key points to keep in mind when describing your works are (1) the type of artist you are, (2) the style you work in, (3) the content of your art as described by your philosophy, and (4) your use of the media. Your goal is to give viewers an idea of what is unique about your work, to pique their interest. Keep your description simple, brief, and honest, whether you are speaking to someone or using the description in printed material.

When writing an "Artist's Statement," keep it to one or two paragraphs and no more than 100 words. Stay away from vague, flowery words that have no real descriptive meaning; avoid words that are in fashion rather than factual. For example, "opulent but subtle texture" sounds really good, but what do those words mean?

Many artists never make an effort to describe their art in words. It is easier for them to say that they can't describe their work and simply push slides or pictures at the person to whom they are showing their work. That approach won't cut it if you want to market yourself successfully. You would be severely limiting your chance to communicate. You must be able to verbally describe your artwork, the media you use, the style you use, and the underlying philosophy of your work. And you must set those words on paper.

Constructive Criticism

QUICK TIP

As long as they spell your name correctly you're okay.

In choosing this profession, you leave yourself open for possible abuse by would-be pseudo-critics. So have thick skin, persevere, and remember, as long as the critics spell your name correctly, you are in good shape. What is important to understand is that many artists have been smeared by art critics throughout their careers. It comes with the territory. Always keep in mind that, *an opinion is only an opinion, but a work of art is a fact,* however good or bad it may be. *Only show your best work.*

In 1987, I received a slamming as a museum director. Our museum organized Rufino Tamayo's first major retrospective exhibition on the West Coast. It was a smashing success, and close to 2,000 people attended the opening. Tamayo told me it was the best opening of his work he had ever attended. Numerous art scholars compared the show to his Guggenheim Retrospective of 1979. One local art critic raved about the show and what an opportunity it had been for so many people to be in the company of such an important artist on opening night. Another local critic, however, panned the show as well as Tamayo, claiming he was a "nobody who could only paint stick figures from south of the border."

Seeking out constructive criticism is an important part of your artistic development. Solicit responses about your work from people you respect, not just from those who will tell you how wonderful your art is. Choose people who will be truthful and are knowledgeable enough to evaluate your works. You may find a fellow artist, instructor, curator, or consultant who will set aside time for you if you ask. Remember that they are helping you, so be gracious, keep an open mind, and listen. It is not the time to argue your philosophy or style but a time to listen to what another person receives from your work. Think about what the person is telling you; later, you may either disregard that view or use it for your own growth.

I do not recommend changing who you are as an artist every time someone comments on your work. One artist friend was so influenced by artistic reviews in the newspaper that he changed his style every week. He changed so often that he never gave himself the opportunity to be recognized for his own good work. As a result, he never fully developed his own style, which was very good. If you create a work that you feel good about, it is important to have conviction in that work. Know what your work is about and what gives you inspiration.

4 MARKETPLACES AND OPPORTUNITIES

Whether modest or extravagant, your ambitions for your work will be best achieved by carefully planning the steps you take to reach your goals. Before marketing your art, you must understand what marketplaces are available. A well-thought-out business and career plan will call for more than one market; therefore, it is important to know all options and possibilities that exist. With this knowledge, you can then select your target markets.

QUICK TIP

Keep an open mind.

Each venue will have its advantages and disadvantages as related to your goals. One venue may give you experience and artistic maturity while another will give you prominence in the art world.

Consider all available options. After doing so, eliminate venues that do not support your career plan. Galleries, museums, and collectors pursue different goals, and some venues may not be appropriate for your art. Qualifying your contacts will uncover their focus, saving you time and frustration.

Each venue falls within one of four categories: local, regional, national, or international. Depending upon your prior exposure and success, I suggest you target markets in that order. Use one level of exhibition to build to the next. If you have only limited exposure and try to jump immediately into the international market, the odds will be against you. As your exposure increases, your network of contacts and support will grow rapidly, as will your success. Build your marketplaces one step at a time.

One artist I worked with recently obtained gallery representation as a result of always being prepared. When leaving for a vacation in the Caribbean, he took along a presentation package of his work, "just in case." The opportunity arose to show his work to a dealer in St. Thomas; after a few brief conversations and a presentation, the dealer offered to represent the artist's work.

Such opportunities for meeting contacts are not limited to artists. One art writer with whom I work struck up a conversation in a Los Angeles hair salon with the woman sitting next to her. As it turned out, the woman was a producer looking for new projects. The writer presented her book, and the producer became interested in the writer's work. That chance conversation has since developed into a business arrangement. As you can see, opportunities can be found almost anywhere.

Fine Art Galleries

A fine art gallery is a business that has as its primary purpose the selling of art for a profit. This type of gallery, however, is more interested in the career and the importance of the artist than are other types of galleries. Fine art galleries generally work on a percentage or consignment basis. Such galleries rarely purchase an artist's works for resale.

Most fine art galleries have a specific type of art on which they focus. One gallery may sell Southwestern art; another, watercolors; and another, contemporary abstracts. A gallery may even limit itself to a specific price range or subject matter. Levels of fine art galleries exist, ranging from promotion of blue chip artists to representation of lesser known artists. It is your job to qualify the galleries based on style, price range, and subject matter of the art they sell.

QUICK TIP

Know the type of gallery your art belongs in.

Even among galleries that sell the same type of art, levels of stature or prominence vary. One gallery may be a commercial art supply store with a small exhibition space in the back; another may be a heavily promoted gallery with a very dedicated dealer. Again, you will learn about the different galleries during the qualification process.

Exhibiting your art in a fine art gallery has many advantages. Your work receives exposure to more people than it would in your studio. Your art also gains credibility and value from the reputation of other artists showing in the gallery.

Galleries have large networks to sell and promote the works of their artists. Because their goal is to increase the importance of your work and thereby increase their sales, the network will be working for you. Openings, receptions, and other events are held to draw more customers. When a buyer is found for a piece, the dealer takes care of it. You won't have to negotiate price or value. You simply receive your percentage of the purchase price.

Selling through dealers does have disadvantages. Because the sales process is out of your hands, you do not meet the people who collect your work. In your agreement with the gallery, be sure to include a clause stipulating that you are to be provided records of the collectors of your work if the gallery goes out of business.

Some galleries are not as aggressive as others in promoting your work. Promotion, however, can be a shared responsibility. If time or financial constraints hinder the gallery from promoting your work, offer to help. Your goal is to break down any barriers—within reason—that stop the gallery from promoting your works. When starting out, consider sharing the cost of invitations or volunteering your time to the gallery. This may make you more attractive to the gallery than another artist. Confirm all arrangements for reimbursement of expenses in writing prior to beginning any work for the gallery. Remember, do not let small issues become barriers to success. Get the exhibition—that is what advances your career.

I believe that in the beginning of an artist's career he or she may have to make compromises. The main thing to remember is that without shows your opportunity for sales, recognition, and building a career will not happen.

Commercial Galleries

A commercial gallery, like its fine art counterpart, has as its primary purpose the selling of art for a profit. Unlike the fine art gallery, it focuses on selling a "product," not necessarily promoting the career of the artist. The works displayed in a commercial gallery are usually consumer-oriented. Most such galleries deal in originals; however, you might see an artist's "product line" of framed prints, unframed prints, greeting cards, T-shirts, and other items for sale. Commercial galleries range from frame shops and boutiques, often showing lesser known artists, to sophisticated galleries exhibiting the works of blue chip artists.

The staff of commercial galleries are salespeople. It is the goal to sell anything that is hanging on the walls. They often know very little about art or even about the artist who created the works they sell. They are not art dealers with networks of serious collectors or institutional contacts. They are only interested in one thing: selling!

If you are concerned primarily with making sales, a commercial gallery can generate revenue on a regular basis. One artist I work with has a gallery in his home town that features his work. He averages $8,000 a month in sales with a product line focused on the tourist trade. His work is priced for the average consumer.

The major advantage of showing in a commercial gallery is increased exposure to the general public and more opportunities for sales. Your works will be shown for a reasonable amount of time, and unsold works will be returned to you. While your work is selling well, the gallery will be very dedicated to you. But continue to expand your product line, because at some point, your work may become less popular. Never become complacent with your current marketplace or product.

Commercial galleries have certain disadvantages. For the fine artist who wishes to promote the importance of his or her work beyond a sale, the gallery will not advance your career with the same dedication as that of the fine art gallery. Blue chip collectors, museums, and universities—the people and institutions who can heavily influence your career—do not buy or show works from this type of gallery. As always, carefully choose your direction and the galleries that represent you.

Even if you are a commercial artist primarily concerned with sales, reliance on a single commercial gallery, will limit your possibilities. At first you may be the primary focus of the gallery. If ownership changes hands or the focus of the gallery changes, your work can move to the back of the gallery. Regardless of the type of gallery that displays your work, frequently check on the gallery to stay current with what is going on with your work.

Gallery Chains

The gallery chain is usually a network of commercial galleries with many exhibition spaces in different locations. These galleries deal with a broad spectrum of artists from the very famous to the lesser known. An established artist gives validity to the chain's stable of artists and keeps the chain's credibility high.

The gallery chains have a more commercial approach than the traditional galleries. They typically handle quality prints of famous artists and heavily advertise and display the prints. Alongside these prints may be an original painting by a lesser known artist. This original painting is often perceived by the public as having a similar value to that of the quality print of the famous artist. This marketing tactic is commonly used to present a relatively unknown artist to less experienced collectors. Thus the gallery takes advantage of the best of both worlds, using the reputation of the established artist to promote the value of the lesser known artist.

A gallery chain can be good for an artist. Because the artist's work receives exposure in a number of geographic locations, opportunity for higher volume of sales exists because of sheer numbers.

QUICK TIP

Be selective about who you deal with.

The final decision to handle an artist's work usually comes from the chain's corporate office. Make sure you can produce enough works, whether originals or prints, to make it worth the gallery chain's time. If you have developed a publishing plan, as discussed in the chapter, "Publishing Your Work," you will probably be able to satisfy the gallery's needs. Keep your options open.

Artist Co-op Galleries

A co-op (cooperative) gallery is where a group of artists have joined to rent exhibition space. The artists share all costs equally for promoting and holding shows, openings, receptions, and similar activities. In turn, profits from sales through this space are also shared. The division of revenue is agreed upon among the artists. If you have not shown much or are having difficulty obtaining representation, a co-op gallery is a viable option.

Co-ops are a good way to show your works in a gallery setting or to learn firsthand about promotions and sales. The next time you show your works, you will have a better understanding of what the gallery must consider.

Location of the gallery is extremely important as are the artists who show there. Check out the other artists by attending their exhibitions and talking to them.

Art Dealers

An art dealer is an essential link between your art and its sale. Art dealers often own or direct galleries and many specialize in specific types of art.

A gallery dealer can be an important influence on your career. The art business is a lot like any business: it's who you know. If you seek exposure in museums, it is important to attain representation by a dealer who is connected to these institutions.

Always remember that a good art dealer will know collectors who can add importance to your work when they purchase it. It is the company your art keeps that enhances its value. When other collectors hear of the purchase, they may become interested in collecting your work.

When you are considering different dealers to represent you, be extremely thorough in your evaluation. Although you need to open avenues of exposure for your art, you must do so with a dealer who has earned a good reputation for his or her work. One of my artist friends had an unfortunate experience with a Dallas gallery. He shipped from California a number of his sculpture pieces to this gallery with a written commitment to exhibit the work for one month.

When he inquired to confirm receipt of the sculpture, no one at the gallery seemed to know anything. Finally, the dealer said the pieces had been damaged in shipping and were useless for the show. This news so alarmed the artist he immediately drove to Dallas. He found the crates had not even been opened. Fortunately, no damage had occurred. The gallery had simply gone out of business and could not live up to its commitments.

The moral of this story is to be selective and thorough in finding the very best dealer you can. Determine the dealer's stability. Look at the dealer's track record. Find out which artists the dealer represents and which collectors buy from the dealer. When you qualify fine art galleries, you will also be qualifying dealers.

Independent Dealers

An independent dealer is an individual who handles the sale of art, often without a gallery or exhibition space. The independent dealer may be a former curator, gallery dealer, or art-related professional. As with the gallery dealer, the independent dealer may focus on a specific type of art.

Independent dealers may rent space for an exhibition. When collaborating with a gallery, independent dealers bring their stable of artists to the gallery for exhibition.

Independent dealers may have excellent networking channels, along with access to collectors, museums, institutions, and other opportunities. Again be selective about those you choose to represent you. Learn about the other artists they represent, who their collectors are, and so forth.

Corporate Art Consultants (Dealers)

The corporate art consultant is a dealer who sells art to companies and institutions. This type of dealer operates much as the gallery dealer does, often having a small gallery space.

The consultant most often works with companies that are expanding, revamping their image, or redecorating their offices. Occasionally, consultants have corporate clients that own important collections for which they act as a curator, developing and selecting works for the collections. These dealers have many projects at one time, which means more opportunities for your work to sell.

Art consultants best represent muralists, portrait painters, and commission artists. Unlike a gallery that holds a solo show once or twice a year, consultants fill the requests of their clientele on a daily basis. These frequent sales can be of major financial benefit to the artists and keep them very busy.

Sales from Your Studio—Caution!

Direct sales from your studio can be very effective. Many collectors like to deal directly with the artist. If you are not represented by a gallery and are willing to do the legwork, I recommend studio sales. It allows people to get to know you and your work. Consider having a studio show once or twice a year. The best times for such shows are from November to early December and in the late spring (but not too close to April 15).

A word of caution: Handle your studio sales diplomatically, or you may lose the gallery representation you worked so hard to attain. If you are represented by a gallery close to your studio, you run a high risk of losing the gallery by competing with rather than supporting its sales efforts. Most galleries frown on artists who sell out of the "back door" of their studios. Once you have a reputation for doing so, galleries will not touch you. Word travels fast in the art world.

One artist in my community sold his work well, although never through gallery representation. I was curious why his work was never in a gallery. Finally I learned that sometime ago his work had been sold in galleries. But after people had seen his work in a gallery, they would go to his studio and buy his work at greatly discounted prices. The local dealers blackballed him.

Artists who are represented by galleries some distance away can successfully sell directly from their studios with the knowledge and consent of their dealer. Such artists, however, should be careful to maintain price integrity and not undercut the prices posted by the galleries. Again, if you sabotage the work the galleries have done to increase the value of your art, you will undoubtedly lose your representation.

If you decide to sell from your studio, consider giving your gallery 5 percent to 10 percent of your sales. This sharing will show that your loyalties remain with the gallery. A dealer would feel comfortable sending a client to meet you, knowing you are honestly collaborating.

Museums

Museums exhibit works of art and provide cultural enrichment to their community. Museums are not there to sell your work, although posters or limited editions may be available in museum stores. A piece on loan from a gallery to a museum may be sold but not removed until after the exhibit is over. The museum may receive a percentage of the sale out of courtesy from the dealer, but again, the museum is not there to sell works of art.

The first impression you make as a professional artist is never more important than when presenting your work to a museum. The key to attaining a museum curator's attention is to present a well-organized package and a strong body of work. The type of presentation package used for a museum should be academic and not commercial.

Each museum has specific types of art on which it focuses. One museum may exhibit regional art of varying styles, while another exhibits contemporary art from Europe.

Alternatively, a museum may limit itself to a specific subject matter, such as Western art. Qualify your target museums on the basis of the work they exhibit.

Even among museums of similar focus, levels of stature or prominence vary. One museum may be a local endeavor with patronage primarily from the surrounding community; another may be a nationally known institution with high visibility. Again, qualify the museum before contacting it about your work.

QUICK TIP

Find out the venue's policies for accepting work.

Exhibiting your work in a museum has may advantages. The foremost advantage is the exhibition enhances your exposure in an academic setting and increases the credibility of your work, demonstrating to the art world that your work has institutional acceptance and importance. Do not refuse to participate in a museum group show in pursuit of a solo show. Group shows with known artists enhance the importance of your art.

Museums also hold openings and receptions to promote exhibitions. These events are well attended and you receive exposure to a well-educated, art-viewing public. Whenever an event is held with your work, you must attend. It is vital to your career to attend and get to know the people who are interested in your art.

Museum curators and directors are important and influential people in the art world. As with art dealers, curators can have a tremendous influence on your career. If curators are supportive of your work, they will promote you to other institutions as well as their own museum for future shows. Curators can also present your work to museum patrons as well as introduce you to their network of contacts.

Museums often have funds for acquisitions to their collection. Keep in mind when selling to a museum that it may expect to receive a reduced price. An artist is honored when a museum or similar institution elects to purchase a piece for its collection. Such a purchase will provide a definite career boost. Also consider donating your work to a museum. Each institution has its own policy regarding what donations it accepts.

Exhibiting in a museum does, however, have a downside. Sales will not occur as they would with a gallery exhibit. And your art will not be available for showing or selling in any other venue until the show is over.

Getting into museums may be a challenge. But you can do it if you realize museums are academic institutions, and therefore you must present your work in an academic manner. Follow the academic instructions provided in chapter 5.

Museum Sales and Rental Galleries

Although a museum's primary focus is the exhibition of art to its community, many museums have sales and rental galleries to place an artist's works with individuals or corporations. The museum usually shares the revenue with the artists whose works have been sold or rented.

In making art available for rent, the museum provides the patron an opportunity either to enjoy a piece without the large initial investment or to take the piece on a trial basis before purchasing. Such rentals can provide the artist with a nominal continuous income. Museums, on average, usually sell 30 percent of rental art. I recommend pursuing the rental option if it is feasible for you.

In targeting museums, ask about their rental-gallery policies. Make sure your art fits the focus of the museum's gallery. You should also inquire about acquisitions, get the name of the gallery director, and learn how artists submit their work for possible sales from the museum's collection.

Traveling Museum Exhibitions

A traveling museum exhibition is a highly organized exhibition of art that travels from one museum to the next. Companies as well as museums organize these exhibitions.

The likelihood of a unestablished artist being selected for one of these traveling exhibitions is very slim. Keep the concept of a traveling exhibition in mind when organizing your presentation materials. You can present your works individually or as a full exhibition, ready to be installed.

I was recently asked to help organize an exhibition of twelve artists in a local gallery. The show was designed around a theme, and the works related to each other based on that focus. The artists shared the costs of producing a forty-eight page catalog. Once the show was hung, I used the exhibition's catalog to present the exhibition to venues outside our local area. As a result, this exhibition was booked into two additional venues. Remember that galleries and institutions like to show exhibits that are well organized because such exhibits reflect positively on their image and require less work and expense.

Curators for Corporate or Private Collections

Corporations and some collectors often hire curators to develop their art collections. A collector, like a gallery or museum, often focuses on a particular artist, period of art, style, subject matter, or other criteria important to the collector.

The curator's job is to enhance the collection, increasing its importance. Purchase of your work by the curator for the collector elevates your importance. Again, remember it is the company your art keeps that influences the importance of your work and your career.

Before approaching a curator, you must know what type of work he or she collects. A good dealer or museum curator can open the door to collectors for you and help prepare you to solicit these types of collectors.

Publishing

Fine art publishing is the process of creating multiple editions of your work through limited editions, mixed media prints, stone lithography, and posters. The goals of publishing are to increase exposure of your art to the public, to open new markets of otherwise unavailable buyers, and to increase the value of your original works by enhancing the recognition of your art. It is my opinion that if you wish to make a living with your art and if your work is suited for it, publishing is a great way to go.

Many fine art publishers are located throughout the country. They are looking for artists whose work has the potential to sell. Publishers often focus on particular styles of art—styles with which they have had success in the past and to which their production and distribution resources are suitable. When you approach a publisher, make sure you know what the publisher printed in the past. Try to learn what the publisher will print in the future. The publisher may be very interested in your work if you have had other editions that have sold well or if you have gained credibility through gallery and museum exhibits.

QUICK TIP

Let the gallery know you are willing to do commission work.

Publishing can be especially useful to the artist whose works require a great deal of time to complete. Many artists believe the financial burden of publishing lies solely with the publisher. Publishers may be more attracted to an artist willing to share the financial risk of producing the artworks, especially if the artist is an unknown with no real track record in publishing. Remember, 100 percent of nothing is nothing.

Commissions

Commissions are specified works of art produced for a given buyer. In essence, you are being paid to work within given guidelines.

Commission work can be financially rewarding, but I would not recommend it for your total income. You can obtain commissions through galleries, art dealers, consultants, and interior designers or through your own studio. If your art fits, commissions can round out your marketing plan and also provide a steady income.

Art Fairs and Shows

Art fairs are a good way for artists who produce decorative art to sell their work directly to the public. If your work is avant-garde, you probably will not find success through these venues. Most successful at art fairs are prolific artists who have produced limited editions of their works. You can be financially well rewarded by virtue of the sheer numbers of people you will come in contact with.

A number of artists I work with concentrate their efforts on art fairs. One artist in particular travels to the fairs almost weekly. He often generates around $5,000 each weekend from sales of originals and prints of his work. Fairs can be lucrative, especially if your work is popular and you are willing to work hard.

These fairs are often sponsored by local or regional art organizations. Many fairs charge a fee as well as take a small percentage of your gross sales. Art fairs are wonderful places to get a reading of how the public responds to your work. Be sure to research if your work is compatible with the other art at a particular fair.

Numerous prestigious and exclusive art shows are held throughout the year. These shows exhibit the very best contemporary fine art as well as commercial art. Exhibitions are by invitation only and usually require a well-connected dealer to be accepted. Visit these shows to see firsthand the art that is making it in the "real world."

Juried Shows and Competitions

A juried show is very much like a gallery show, only the pieces being exhibited are reviewed and judged against one another by a panel of professionals from the art community. A juried show may be sponsored by a museum, local university, nonprofit organization, governmental, or civic group.

The purpose of entering a competition is to gain acceptance from the art world rather than close a sale. Earning a juried award serves to validate your artistic importance to the art community. Your art may sell by virtue of your work's exposure during the competition, but sales are not the primary focus.

Winning a juried competition requires a bit of strategy. First, select the type of competition that is compatible with the art you create. Also, if you know who the judges are, you can enhance your chances of winning by selecting works that appeal to their taste.

One disadvantage to juried competitions is that you have absolutely no input or control over the outcome. This lack of control can be frustrating, but keep in mind that visibility of your work is most important feature of juried shows.

Locating juried shows is easy. Keep abreast of activities by going to college exhibitions, gallery shows, local museums, art supply stores, and similar places. Ask about any upcoming competitions. You can also learn about juried shows from art magazines, many of which list such competitions, and from arts organizations, which usually provide their members with information about competitions.

Some competitions charge a fee to process your work. If the fees are reasonable, it may be worth your time and energy to enter. An artist I know asked my opinion about whether she should enter an exhibition in Japan. The entry fee was $300 and the show was accepting only 20 artists from among 300 to 400 entries. I asked her which artists had been selected in the past. She read the list, and it was composed of the standard blue chip regulars. My advice to her was to keep her $300, buy more supplies for new works, and look for competitions that were not so likely to be politically influenced. I do not mean to discourage you, but the art world is very political. If you are not dealing within a given political arena, you may find yourself on the outside looking in.

Schools and Universities

Schools and universities are venues that nonstudent artists often disregard. They believe these institutions are open only to students. Schools have schedules of shows, exhibitions, and competitions throughout the year to which artists not affiliated with the institutions may submit their work. Shows in such institutions are worthwhile venues, as they add another academic credential to your biography. These exhibitions present your work to students, faculty, the public, and the media. Art critics often attend such shows.

State and County Fairs

Throughout the country, state and county fairs showcase a variety of interests including the arts—most often the commercial arts. A fair can be a good place to gain further exposure and it gives you an avenue to learn about the public's reaction to your art. Many large fairs hold juried competitions in a variety of categories and allow the artists to sell their works.

One artist I worked with in the past showed his art every year at the Los Angeles County Fair. Not only did he receive a number of commissions as well as inquiries from galleries from showing his work at the fair, more than 150,000 people viewed his art.

If you are interested in showing at a fair, contact the appropriate state or county fairgrounds or agricultural commission to obtain an application form.

Fund-raisers

It is my strong belief that all artists should contribute at least a few of their works to one or two fund-raising events every year. Fund raisers are socially conscious activities that not only expose your works to the public but also benefit worthwhile causes.

Museum auctions are best for donating your work because those who attend already have a love for the arts. The list of philanthropic fund-raisers is endless. Some organizations will ask for a total donation, and some will give a percentage back to the artist. Contact the organization to find out what its policies are.

QUICK TIP

Keep your work in front of the public.

Call your local museums and ask for information on their annual auction fund-raiser and what their policies are for accepting works.

Corporate Loans

Artists, dealers, galleries, and museums sometimes approach large companies and institutions and offer them artworks on loan, often for a nominal fee. This arrangement allows the organizations to hang quality works of art and project a successful image without incurring purchase costs. For the artist, the loan provides modest revenue and a storage space for a work of art.

Some organizations will ask you to lend a piece without reimbursement. You may wish to give such a loan some consideration. You never know who may see your work on display at the company and, in turn, purchase one of your works. For such displays, select strong pieces, but not necessarily those you may want to exhibit in a gallery or museum in the near future.

Please note that it is imperative to have a clearly written signed agreement specifying your retained ownership of the art and the terms by which the loan will be governed. Include a clause that allows you to terminate the loan should a buyer or exhibition for the piece be found. You may reserve the right to substitute a piece upon the approval of the other party. Refer to the sample loan document provided in the appendix.

Religious Organizations

Religious organizations can provide a positive venue for your work. Shows hosted by such organizations draw attention to your works not only within the congregation but also often through the local media.

I recently was asked to exhibit my works at a Southern California church. My art challenges religious and social beliefs, both positively and negatively. The exhibition created controversy within the church, which served to heighten the exposure of the work; 5,000 people attended the exhibit's opening, which was held on a Sunday. Virtually every person attending church services was exposed to the work. It was one of my most interesting exhibitions because of the responses from the audience.

Each faith has its guidelines for appropriateness of exhibiting works of art within its halls of worship. Before approaching a religious venue, understand the guidelines and assess your work in this light.

Libraries

Libraries are another interesting venue to pursue. Libraries educate the communities they serve and often organize art shows focusing on a certain style, era, or social issue. Art organizations that do not have their own space frequently use libraries for shows. Contact your local libraries for a schedule of exhibitions they are planning. If the libraries do not have any exhibits planned, you may wish to propose a show for them. If you have already developed a concept for a traveling show, you will be ready to make such an offer. You may even wish to lend or donate a piece to the library for display.

Restaurants, Bars, and Other Public Businesses

Artists, dealers, galleries, and museums may approach a variety of places open to the public, such as restaurants and bars, with artworks available for display at little or no cost. You could, for example, offer a restaurant an opportunity to hang some of your work. The restaurant can project a successful image without spending money to purchase the art. For the artist, the display can generate income and provide exposure of the works to the public that may lead to sales and other opportunities. Everyone involved in such an arrangement can win.

When your work is on display in a business, be sure to provide information sheets with your or your dealer's telephone number and address. Also make sure that your works are delivered on time and that you are present when the work is unveiled. Public businesses are good venues for pre-exhibition promotions.

Interior Designers

Interior designers are always looking for art to use in their projects. Such use increases exposure of your work because a good designer often has many jobs going at one time.

Interior designers are also good sources for commission works. Designers often search for a work of art that will enhance a room. The work will most likely be selected for its decorative value rather than for its artistic importance.

Trading/Barter

Many artists exchange their works for needed services—everything from photography, printing, and legal work to computers, jewelry, and so on. One artist I know trades art each year for meal coupons at fine restaurants throughout the community. These trades, he explains, enable him to dine economically at the same restaurants his collectors frequent.

Internet Site

There are many opportunities for marketing your art on the Internet and World Wide Web. By establishing an effective and professional site, you have the ability to reach a diverse audience that includes galleries, museums, publishers, and private collectors. If you decide to establish a presence in cyberspace, it's important to have your site designed by professionals who specialize in the marketing of art and artists.

Focus on the Long-term Goals of Your Career Plan

QUICK TIP

Keep your plan rolling.

Whatever path you choose for your career, it is important to remain consistent in your plan, choosing marketplaces and opportunities that complement each other. Carefully choose your direction and those who represent you. Always keep your goals and plan in mind as you promote, exhibit, and sell your work.

As an example, artists who sell their work in commercial galleries will have a difficult time promoting their work to museums. However, artists who sell their work through fine art galleries can more easily move into museums because their works have not been perceived as "commercial" even though they have been for sale.

Do not let the allure of the easy dollar overshadow your ultimate goals. If an opportunity does not fit into your overall career plan, it is best to turn it down. If you do not, you will become your career's own worst enemy, having created inconsistencies in the identity of you and your art. There is nothing wrong with choosing to be a commercial artist. Simply remember that once you have made that choice, it will be difficult to then take your work back into the fine art arena. Develop your plan based upon your long-term goals, then devote all your activities to implementing your plan and achieving your goals.

EXAMPLE: MARKET SELECTION WORKSHEET

This worksheet lists all the potential markets for your art. The applicability of each venue for the fine arts or the commercial arts is noted in the two columns to the right.

Rank the priority of each selected venue within your career goals by: 1—highest priority, 2—moderate priority, 3—low priority, and 4—would be nice if it fits in. This ranking will establish the order in which you will address the venue as you begin carrying out your plan.

Market		Order of Priority	Fine Art Venue	Commercial Art Venue
✓	Fine Arts Gallery	*1*	*X*	
	Commercial Gallery		*X*	*X*
	Gallery Chain		*X*	*X*
	Co-op Gallery		*X*	*X*
✓	Art Dealer	*1*	*X*	*X*
✓	Independent Art Dealer	*2*	*X*	*X*
✓	Corporate Art Consultant	*3*	*X*	*X*
✓	Studio Sales (Caution!)	*1*	*X*	*X*
✓	Museums	*1*	*X*	
✓	Museum Sales/Rental Gallery	*2*	*X*	
	Traveling Museum Shows		*X*	
✓	Curator for Collections	*1*	*X*	
✓	Publishing	*2*	*X*	*X*
	Commissions		*X*	*X*
	Art Fairs and Shows		*X*	*X*
	Juried Shows and Competitions		*X*	*X*
✓	Schools and Universities	*2*	*X*	*X*
	State and County Fairs		*X*	*X*
✓	Fund-raisers	*1*	*X*	*X*
	Corporate Loans		*X*	*X*
✓	Religious Groups	*4*	*X*	*X*
	Libraries		*X*	*X*
	Restaurants, Bars, etc.		*X*	*X*
	Interior Designers		*X*	*X*
	Trade/Barter		*X*	*X*
	Internet Site		*X*	*X*

5 DEVELOPING YOUR PRESENTATION MATERIALS

QUICK TIP

Be sure your presentation is professional.

This chapter is the single most important one in the book. Simply put, without your presentation materials, you are out of business. As you develop your work and knowledge during your career, you must continually update your presentation materials. These materials will often be the only communication between yourself and a potential exhibition or sale.

The presentation package speaks both of you and for you. Remember, when one person meets another, first impressions occur within the initial five seconds and at least 70 percent of that first impression relies on nonverbal factors. The same is true when a person first sees your presentation materials. This chapter shows you how to ensure your materials work effectively on your behalf.

Follow the examples described in this chapter to develop a presentation that will represent you and your work in the best possible light.

Commercial versus Academic

The presentation of commercial art differs from that of fine art. Although materials for academic fine art presentations can also be used for commercial presentation, the reverse is not true.

Commercial materials cannot be used in an academic venue. Commercial materials are designed to sell the artist and to generate revenue. Academic materials promote the importance of the art—the historical comparison to other important works and the significance of the artist's development to the art world. Written material for a fine art presentation should be prepared by an art writer or other professional with a knowledge of art and art history. Do not write about yourself.

Commercial materials are usually slick sales tools. Commercial pieces use strong adjectives as shown in the first example on page 68. In contrast, an academic statement emphasizes the art rather than the artist, as shown in the second example on page 72.

The presentation materials in this book are based on the academic approach. They can serve you well in both academic and commercial venues.

Don't Let Your Presentation Materials Outshine Your Work

This statement is simple but true. The works of art shown in your materials must be your strongest pieces. When you select works for inclusion in your presentation materials, it might be wise to have a knowledgeable art professional evaluate your present works and help you select your best pieces. You may find that you need to create a number of stronger pieces to round out your presentation. Always select your pieces before you begin developing your materials.

The Total Package

You will develop two presentation packages; one will be a pared-down version of the other. The complete package will be your master archive, consisting of all presentation materials, résumés, promotional materials, invitations, newspaper and magazine reviews, referral letters, slides, and photographs pertaining to your work. This archive will be the chronological record of your development as an artist.

QUICK TIP

Select works that are consistent.

From the archive, you will select items to create the academic presentation materials that you will use to build your career. When soliciting galleries, museums, or other venues, for example, you will present only those materials pertinent to each venue's needs. In time, if there is ever a retrospective of your work, the exhibitor may want to delve into the entirety of your archive.

The formats provided here are by no means the only correct approaches. They are, however, those with which I have repeatedly obtained success. You may come across new approaches that will work for you. Don't be afraid to incorporate them into your presentation. Remember, however, that these materials are to be academic in style and content, not commercial.

Selecting the Works to Present

A complete presentation should feature your very best work. Choose pieces consistent with one another. Showing a variety of styles does not demonstrate the scope of your skills. Such a presentation will damage your potential for representation by failing to indicate which style is yours. Unless your current works have strong ties to earlier works, avoid showing the two together. Remember, if you want to be taken seriously, you must present a single body of work that has strength and continuity and shows a well-defined sense of direction.

How do you select the best pieces to present? The first step is to review photographs or slides of your current works. Always photograph each piece when completed as a record for your archive. From this group, select those works that you feel are the strongest. Consider the availability of each piece for exhibition or for reproduction in a catalog or brochure. If a work has been sold, ask the owner if you can borrow it for photography or exhibition. Most, but not all, owners will agree, but don't assume that you can use it. Always photograph your work.

If you do not feel secure in what you have selected, elicit the aid of a dealer, curator, consultant, knowledgeable art professionals, or FACT's Artist Evaluation Service. Select someone you respect. Explain that you are developing presentation materials and that you value his or her opinion. Most people are more than willing to give you their time and their opinions.

Photographing the Works to Present

The next step in developing your presentation materials is to evaluate the quality of the photographs you have. Content, contrast, and clarity are critical to how well the image will reproduce. Do not cut corners with photographs—they serve as your "spokesperson" to the art community.

Pay a professional photographer to shoot your work. Professional photography can be expensive, but you may be able to find a quality photographer who will trade his or her work for your art. Also consider contacting a local school, as photography students with quality equipment may be willing to work for the experience. I strongly recommend using a 2-1/4" or 4" x 5" format camera. If your only alternative is a 35 mm camera, use a high quality lens, slow speed film, and a tripod to get as crisp an image as possible.

There are guidelines to follow in photographing your works. Present the art alone; no other objects should be present in the image. With the exception of installation shots, avoid showing ceiling or floor lines. The size of a piece will be established by a label applied to the print or slide within the catalog or directly in installation shots. Paintings should be photographed unframed. Sculptures may be photographed with a background but the image should not be cluttered. The focus must be solely on the art object.

Required Photographic Images and Negatives

It is not necessary to have prints made from all your negatives. At a minimum, produce a 35 mm color slide (properly labeled) for all pieces. For work you print, use a 2-1/4" or 4" x 5" format color transparency if at all possible, although 35 mm slides can also be used. The larger format negatives produce better results.

Have one 8" x 10" glossy color print for each of the three strongest images you present in your package. One or two 8" x 10" glossy black-and-white prints should be made from each of two additional images. Contrast in black-and-white photographs is important for quality reproduction in printed press and promotional materials. In total, you will need five copies of each image; one for each of four presentation packages and another for your master archive.

Before you go to print, be sure of your image selections. Once you set the printing process into motion, you are spending precious dollars.

Compiling Your Presentation Package

Assembling an academic presentation package is simple. You have already selected and photographed your very strongest images and are confident your selections are correct. Now you will begin preparing the other materials needed to complete your presentation package.

WRITTEN COMMUNICATIONS

The written word can provide great strength to your presentation. It is important for you to be aware of how to write a proper professional letter. Many good books on letter writing are available. These books provide the grammatical and structural guidelines appropriate for such communication. Invest a few dollars in one of these books and keep it at your desk for reference. A number of examples of artist's letters are included in this book.

QUICK TIP

Keep it short and to the point.

This chapter highlights writing professional cover letters, follow up letters, thank-you notes and résumés—the key writing you will need to undertake in your marketing plan. Writing for the purposes of promotion, such as press releases, will be covered in the section on promotions.

Stationery

The writing papers used in a presentation are simple, clean, and professional. You can find the guidelines for formatting letterhead in any business writing book but, in summary, your name, complete address, telephone number and facsimile number, if any, should be centered at the top of the page. Avoid using flamboyant logos or unusual type style. These devices only clutter your presentation. This conservative style may seem boring, but it is appropriate.

Use a good quality paper. Avoid onion skin, erasable typing paper, and the like. A 20-pound bond is quite effective. White or soft cream papers are the most appropriate; other colors, again, can appear too flashy. A standard 8-1/2" x 11" sheet size is proper. Do not use the slightly smaller personal sheet, which would be smaller than the overall size of the presentation package.

The mailing envelope for your presentation package should be slightly larger than the presentation itself to avoid bending the photographs and catalog. Use an envelope that is slightly padded to protect the package. Envelopes for follow-up letters not accompanied by materials should match the size, color, and type of paper on which the original cover letter was printed.

Check Your Spelling and Grammar

Once you have gone to the effort to create a good letter, it is imperative to check the grammar and spelling. If you do not feel confident in your ability to do so, have someone else proofread the letter for spelling and typographical errors. Few things are less professional than mailing a letter with typos and misspellings. This added step will save you from embarrassment.

Confirm that you have used the correct spelling of the recipient's name, title, and business before sending the letter. If you are unsure, make another call to confirm that your information is correct. When this information is right, people tend not to notice, but when it is wrong, it sticks out like a sore thumb.

Fonts and Printing

Given today's age of computers, I strongly suggest that all letters be printed on some type of laser printer. The quality of laser printing is superior to that of dot matrix printers or typewriters. If you do not have a laser printer, you can go to almost any copy center or word processing service and rent time on computers. The rental fee is modest, and the laser printing greatly enhances your presentation. If you feel you cannot afford a laser printing service, at least use a typewriter. Again, do not handwrite your letters except for possibly thank-you notes.

In printing out your letter, use a font that is contemporary, clean, and easy to read. As you avoided using creative logos on the letterhead, refrain from using stylized fonts that may be difficult to read. Your goal is to communicate clearly.

Length of a Letter

The very best letters are short and to the point. Begin with a complimentary opening statement or mention the name of a mutual acquaintance—something to attract interest. After the opening, move directly to your letter. Refrain from using flowery language and lengthy sentences. Keep your sentences short and simple.

Standardizing Your Letter Library

It is important for you to create your own library of commonly used letters, including standard cover letters for each venue type, follow-up letters and thank-you notes. When the time comes to mail to a prospective venue, select the letter that is most appropriate for the situation. Inset the address of the venue and make the necessary changes in the body of the letter. Once you have established a letter library, you will spend less time sending out packages.

Please be sure to understand that I do not mean for you to photocopy a slew of standard, nondirected letters starting with "Dear Venue." Each letter must be specifically addressed to the recipient of the letter. Your library should contain standardized versions for different situations.

Keep Files of All Communications

As with the archive of all your presentation materials, it is important for you to keep a record of all communications coming in and going out of your studio. Each time you send a letter, make a copy of it for yourself. Create a filing system so that you can track the letters you send and the responses you receive. One of the most effective methods is to label a file folder for each venue you are soliciting, place all communications and information into that file, and then store each file in alphabetical order in a filing drawer. This system will make the file quickly accessible any time you are either writing to or talking with that venue. Organization of your office communications is one of the keys to success.

Format of the Page

The format of a business letter is quite simple, as shown on the following pages. Keep to this format unless you find another in your reference that is more suited to your writing style.

Feedback about Your Letter Writing

Writing a good business letter is a developed skill for most people. Business writing requires practice and observation. Keep track of your letters that elicit the most positive responses from the recipients. If you have created an unusually effective letter, put it in your library and use it again.

PRESENTATION MATERIALS

Cover Letter

The presentation cover letter introduces you and your art to the prospective venue. It is placed on top of all other materials in the presentation package and is the first impression you make. It is a letter of introduction and request for action that is personalized for each recipient. You will never receive the desired results from an impersonal, generic cover letter. (For samples of effective cover letters, please refer to the end of this chapter.)

All printed materials should be laser printed in a clean, contemporary type style. Avoid italic, gothic, and other ornate fonts that detract from the simplicity of the presentation. Handwritten cover letters are unacceptable. A typed letter is adequate, but lacks the impression created by a laser-printed letter. You may not own a laser printer, but access to one is easy. Check with secretarial services or large copying shops. Most of these businesses provide the required computer services.

Effective Cover Letters

The presentation cover letter reintroduces you and your art to the prospective venue, and it should arrive at the venue immediately after your initial solicitation and introductory telephone call. Remember, never send unsolicited materials. When you write a cover letter proposing your presentation, keep the recipient's needs in mind.

The opening paragraph will remind the recipient of your earlier phone call. If you were referred by someone who may be important to the venue, state this in the opening.

In the second paragraph make a specific statement about your work. Be brief—discuss strengths of your art and your exhibition experience. Point out the link between your art and the venue's goals and focus.

The final paragraph is a request for action. What would you like the venue to do? Be clear about your intention. Plan what actions need to be taken and ask to take the first step. This step may be meeting the recipient of the letter at his or her location or having the recipient visit your studio. As the saying goes, if you do not ask, you will not receive.

You may find other outlines for your cover letters that suit your style and personality more closely. The following examples are those that have been successful for me. The focus of these letters was derived from initial telephone contact. Above all, use letters that work for you. Use the Presentation Cover Letter Worksheet in the appendix to create two or three letters for your library.

Assembling the Presentation Package

Place the items on top of one another, with the cover letter on top and return envelope on the bottom. Make sure each element faces up. You want the recipient of your package to see your cover letter first. The package should not bend. You may wish to insert clean cardboard on both sides of your materials.

Address the envelope using a laser-printed or typed mailing label. Include the name of the recipient, his or her title, name of the organization, and complete address with ZIP code. If you are unsure about any information on the label, call to verify. Also put a return address label on the envelope. A rubber stamp or sticker that reads "Photographs Enclosed—Do Not Bend" will help protect the package.

The presentation materials are now complete and ready to send to your target venue. Prepare at least four complete sets of your master presentation package, more if you will be soliciting actively. Keep track of who has each of your presentation packages. Create a tracking system so you can ask for the package back when the recipient has reviewed your works. Refer to the section on presenting your work for further information on properly presenting your materials and keeping track of who has what.

Note that it is important to keep your master presentation package intact. Do not let anyone borrow any part of it, and never use it yourself for presentations. The master package is used only to make duplicates.

***EXAMPLE:* COVER LETTER WITH PERSONAL REFERRAL—FOR A GALLERY**

Ms. Michelle Talvison
1556 South Watkins Drive
Los Angeles, CA 90046
(213) 555-1212

January 1, 1997

Mr. Mathew Hillsing
Director
Sonova Gallery
408 Greene Street
New York, NY 10012

Dear Mathew:

It was a pleasure speaking with you this morning. As I mentioned, one of your collectors, Carol Carlotel, suggested I contact you. After personally reviewing my work, she thought the style, strength, and media in my work would be interesting to you and very salable through your gallery.

My work has been widely exhibited on the West Coast and Pacific Rim, including the Mockteller Museum in San Francisco, the Alternative Museum in Los Angeles, and the Modern Museum in San Diego. Several of your collectors have purchased my work over the past few years and have expressed continued interest in acquiring new pieces. They all have told me that they were attracted to my painting by my unique use of color and found objects that lures viewers into the painting.

Mathew, I have enclosed presentation materials for your review, including a catalog from my current show at the Blumschmelt Gallery. I will call you again next week to discuss the possibility of your gallery representing my work.

Sincerely,

Michelle Talvison

Encl. Presentation Materials

EXAMPLE: COVER LETTER WITHOUT PERSONAL REFERRAL—FOR A GALLERY

Ms. Kelly Bryson
3502 Brookshire Glen
Los Angeles, CA 90046
(213) 555-1236

January 1, 1997

Mr. Mathew Hillsing
Director
Sonova Gallery
408 Greene Street
New York, NY 10012

Dear Mathew:

It was a pleasure speaking with you this morning. As I mentioned, I have recently seen your advertisements in various national art magazines and have been impressed with the quality of work you represent. I am interested in exposure of my work on the East Coast and believe the style, strength, and media of my art may be interesting to you and very salable through your gallery.

My strong use of color with symbolism is reminiscent of the paintings of Resnick and Newman. I am serious about my career and am interested in working with a dealer such as you not only to accomplish my goals but to help you accomplish yours.

Mathew, I have enclosed presentation materials for your review. I will call you again next week to discuss the possibility of your gallery representing my work.

Sincerely,

Kelly Bryson

Encl. Presentation Materials

** This letter is an example of how entry-level artists can present their work for the first time and create credibility without exposing their inexperience.*

***EXAMPLE:* COVER LETTER WITH PERSONAL REFERRAL—FOR A MUSEUM**

Ms. Michelle Talvison
1556 South Watkins Drive
Los Angeles, CA 90046
(213) 555-1212

January 1, 1997

Ms. Catherine Kingston
Curator
The Contemporary Museum
5504 Broad Street
Los Angeles, CA 90046

Dear Catherine:

It was a pleasure speaking with you this morning. As I mentioned, Robert Gaffey, a board member of your museum, suggested I contact you. After personally visiting my exhibition at the Rothkeller Institute, he felt the style, media, and subject matter of my work ties directly into the focus of your museum.

My work has been widely exhibited on the West Coast and Pacific Rim, including the Mockteller Museum in San Francisco, the Alternative Museum in Los Angeles, and the Modern Museum in San Diego. The intensity of my paintings has been compared to that of Richter, Michaels, and Bellington. Each piece addresses issues confronting society today.

Catherine, I have enclosed presentation materials for your review, including a catalog from my current show at the Blumschmelt Gallery. I will call you again next week to discuss your response to my work and your interest in the possibility of an exhibition.

Sincerely,

Michelle Talvison

Encl. Presentation Materials

EXAMPLE: COVER LETTER WITHOUT PERSONAL REFERRAL—FOR A MUSEUM

Ms. Michelle Talvison
1556 South Watkins Drive
Los Angeles, CA 90046
(213) 555-1212

January 1, 1997

Ms. Catherine Kingston
Curator
The Contemporary Museum
5504 Broad St.
Los Angeles, CA 90046

Dear Catherine:

It was a pleasure speaking with you this morning. As I mentioned, I recently attended the opening of your Brockmeyer Retrospective where I observed that the style, media, and subject matter of my work ties directly into the focus of your museum.

My work has been widely exhibited on the West Coast and Pacific Rim, including the Mockteller Museum in San Francisco, the Alternative Museum in Los Angeles, and the Modern Museum in San Diego. The intensity of my paintings has been compared to that of Richter, Michaels, and Bellington. Each piece addresses issues confronting society today.

Catherine, I have enclosed presentation materials for your review, including a catalog from my current show at the Blumschmelt Gallery. I will call you again next week to discuss your response to my work and your interest in the possibility of an exhibition.

Sincerely,

Michelle Talvison

Encl. Presentation Materials

EXAMPLE: **PRESENTATION COVER LETTER WORKSHEET**

Date *January 1, 1997*

Name *Mathew Hillsing*

Title *Director*

Venue *Sonova Gallery*

Address *408 Greene St.*

City, State, ZIP *New York, NY 10012*

Dear *Mathew*

Opening Paragraph

(Remind Phone Call)

It was a pleasure speaking with you this morning. As I mentioned, one of your collectors, Carol Carlotel, suggested I contact you.

(Presenting Your Art)

After personally reviewing my work, she thought the style, strength, and media in my work would be interesting to you and very salable through your gallery.

Second Paragraph

(Strength of Your Art)

My work has been widely exhibited on the West Coast and Pacific Rim, including the Mockteller (SF), Alternative Museum (LA), and Modern Museum (SD).

(Tie-in Statement)

A number of your collectors have purchased my work over the past few years and have expressed continued interest in acquiring new pieces. They all have told me that they were attracted to my painting by my unique use of color and found objects that lures viewers into the painting.

Closing Paragraph

(Call to Action)

I have enclosed presentation materials for your review, including a catalog from my current show at the Blumschmelt Gallery.

(Your Follow-up Step)

I will call you again next week to discuss the possibility of your gallery representing my work.

Sincerely,

(Your Name)

Michelle Talvison

Follow-up Letters

The purpose of a follow-up letter is to keep the communication lines open and your prospect moving positively from one step to the next. The nature of this letter will be determined by the response or lack of response you have received from your initial contacts with the prospective venue.

Within four days of sending or presenting your materials, make a follow-up call. Your presence on the phone will bring you to the forefront of the person's mind. You will be able to assess his or her impressions of your work. Even though the recipient may not have had a chance to review your work thoroughly, your interaction over the telephone with this person will make an impression.

QUICK TIP

Be friendly and positive.

This follow-up call can also be used to ensure that your package was received by the proper person. If your package has not been received, it is worth your while to track it down. Many artists will pay the additional expense of using an express mail service just for the service's ability to track packages.

After making your follow-up call, write a brief letter. You should create three basic types of follow-up letters for your library, as described below.

1. Soliciting a Response

This type of letter is designed to solicit a response in cases in which the package has been received but not yet reviewed. This letter will restate the second and third paragraphs of your cover letter in a bit more depth. This follow-up letter is again selling your art as something worth the other's time and interest to pursue.

2. The Positive Response Follow-up

This type of letter is designed to maintain the venue's interest in your art. When you have received a positive response from the venue, following a personal meeting, for example, it is important to put down in writing the agreements or proposed plans that were discussed. Your letter should briefly restate the substance of the discussion. Close the letter with a statement of what happens next. If you were asked to provide further information or materials, enclose them with this letter.

Whenever you are dealing with a venue and commitments have been made to you orally, it is imperative that you confirm these commitments in writing. You never know when your contact person will move on in his or her career and be replaced by someone else. You need to obtain a binding agreement, signed by both the venue and yourself. Far too many artists have lost exhibitions because they lacked written commitments.

3. The Negative Response Follow-up

This type of letter is used following a negative response from a venue. As you learned earlier, it is your job to turn a negative response into something positive. Use this letter to gain referrals from the venue. This letter should be a gracious close to your pursuit of the venue, leaving the door open at a future date and a chance for you to obtain names of the people who, in this person's professional opinion, would be worth your while to contact. Remember to accept a negative response graciously. Do not badger people who aren't amenable to selling or showing your work in their venue.

EXAMPLE: FOLLOW-UP LETTER—SOLICITING A RESPONSE

Ms. Michelle Talvison
1556 South Watkins Drive
Los Angeles, CA 90046
(213) 555-1212

January 5, 1997

Mr. Mathew Hillsing
Director
Sonova Gallery
408 Greene Street
New York, NY 10012

Dear Mathew:

Thank you for your compliments regarding the promptness of my response to your request for materials. As you will see, I have enclosed a catalog from one of my recent exhibitions. The essay in the catalog was written by the noted art critic Linda Brock.

My work has received wide acclaim through numerous exhibitions on the West Coast and Pacific Rim, including the Mockteller Museum in San Francisco, the Alternative Museum in Los Angeles, and the Modern Museum in San Diego. A number of your collectors have purchased my work over the past few years and have expressed continued interest in acquiring new pieces. They have all told me that they were attracted to my painting by my unique use of color and found objects that lures viewers into the painting. This uniqueness has created a willingness in the collectors to pay an exceptional price for my work.

Mathew, I will call you again next week to talk about the possibility of your gallery representing my work. I look forward to discussing the mutual benefits of such an association.

Sincerely,

Michelle Talvison

***EXAMPLE:* FOLLOW-UP LETTER—POSITIVE RESPONSE**

Ms. Michelle Talvison
1556 South Watkins Drive
Los Angeles, CA 90046
(213) 555-1212

January 5, 1997

Mr. Mathew Hillsing
Director
Sonova Gallery
408 Greene Street
New York, NY 10012

Dear Mathew:

The opportunity you have presented to exhibit my work in your upcoming group exhibition is very exciting. I am confident my work will help further your reputation for exhibiting and selling quality art.

As we discussed, I will consign the pieces *The Depth of Conscious* and *Grand Illusion* to your gallery for the length of the show, March 15 through April 12, 1997. During that time, you will have the exclusive right to represent and sell these works. If the pieces are not sold during that time, you will ship and insure the pieces back to my studio by April 19. I have enclosed a signed copy of the consignment agreement we reviewed that confirms these arrangements.

Mathew, I am presently arranging for the crating and shipment of these works so that they arrive at your gallery on March 12 as you requested. I will contact you next week with the details regarding jointly producing a group catalog for this exhibition, just as I did for my recent solo exhibition.

Sincerely,

Michelle Talvison

Encl. Signed Consignment Agreement

EXAMPLE: FOLLOW-UP LETTER—NEGATIVE RESPONSE

Ms. Michelle Talvison
1556 South Watkins Drive
Los Angeles, CA 90046
(213) 555-1212

January 5, 1997
Mr. Mathew Hillsing
Director
Sonova Gallery
408 Greene Street
New York, NY 10012

Dear Mathew:

Thank you for reviewing the presentation of my work. Your suggestion to contact Lou Mac to investigate publishing a mixed media limited edition of the two pieces *The Depth of Conscious* and *Grand Illusion* interests me. As a gesture of thanks should an edition be produced, I would like to offer you first choice of a piece for your gallery.

Mathew, if you know of any other people who might be interested in my work, I would greatly appreciate the contact. I will keep in touch and let you know of the progress of my career. I genuinely enjoyed our conversations.

Sincerely,

Michelle Talvison

Thank-you Notes

Thank-you notes are appropriate for all occasions. Always remember to extend a word of thanks to those with whom you come in contact. Such a note is appropriate whether the response you receive is positive or negative, especially after personal presentations. Don't go overboard, but be sure to thank those who have taken their time to help you.

QUICK TIP

Communication will keep things moving in a positive direction.

Constant Communications

Many artists have found that they can receive rapid success by using a constant communication network with the art community. These artists regularly send out information in the form of letters, invitations, notes, and similar communications to keep their collectors and those who are helpful to their career informed of what is happening. Artists who communicate regularly generate name recognition in their targeted markets and the media. Never let too much time pass before sharing the good news of what is happening with your art with others.

The Artist's Statement

An artist's statement is a brief explanation of your philosophy and message. This statement should be brief and to the point, but not so esoteric that the audience is lost. The use of an artist's statement in a catalog is optional. If your statement adds credibility, include it. Including a photograph of yourself in the catalog is also optional. Avoid using superfluous notes, poetry, diary pages, and the like. In an academic catalog, all these personal touches detract from the primary goal: advancing your credibility as an artist.

Ineffective Artist Statements

Esoteric Artist Statement

I try to delve into the inner thoughts of my imagination, always reflecting upon the inner quadrants of my soul to transform reality, searching the innermost recesses of my life. My intensity and commitment to spiritual growth allow my work to be a beacon focused on transformation.

Misfocused Artist Statement

Arthur Smith was born in West Virginia and has lived there most of his life. Over the years he has made a living making furniture for the design industry. Arthur has been married for thirteen years and is the father of three children. Weekends, he enjoys playing golf and fly-fishing. He began painting in high school and has continued to do so for nearly twenty years. The beautiful colors and subtle compositions are accentuated by hand carved frames. His paintings are exhibited in several galleries throughout the South.

Focused and Effective Artist Statement

Arthur Smith has lived in West Virginia most of his life. His artwork is inspired by his surroundings, and he often works from photographs of people and places he visits in the

West Virginia countryside. Smith paints in oils exclusively and works in the style of the plein air painters of the 1930s such as Bischoff, Payne, and Wendt. He is influenced by the beauty and simplicity of what he observes and feels that his art is an accurate reflection of the times in which we live. Smith's work is represented in several important collections.

CATALOG AND BROCHURE

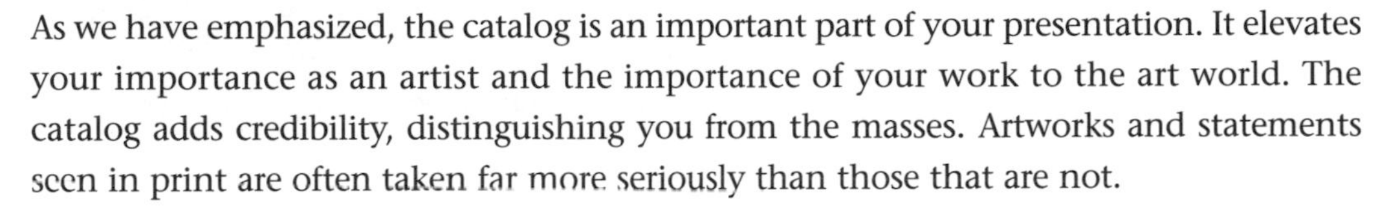

As we have emphasized, the catalog is an important part of your presentation. It elevates your importance as an artist and the importance of your work to the art world. The catalog adds credibility, distinguishing you from the masses. Artworks and statements seen in print are often taken far more seriously than those that are not.

Artists often perceive the need for a catalog but feel it is out of their financial reach. This misconception is unfortunate. By following the guidelines contained in this book for designing an academic catalog and shopping around for production and printing, you can produce a professional catalog with only a modest investment. But if you still feel your budget will not let you create a catalog at this time, consider a brochure like the sample enclosed with this book (see page 91). The brochure has the same elements as the catalog, although in a scaled-down version, and is still an effective promotional piece.

In this chapter, you will learn how to properly design both a catalog and a brochure. Paste in each element as you finish preparing it. Use it as an aid to understand fully each point of design discussed in this chapter. Use the finished product to help you obtain bids from printers, showing them what you are aiming to achieve.

The Total Catalog

An academic catalog or brochure should include a cover, an academic essay, the artist's statement, art images, artist's biography, and catalog design and production credits. A short biography of the catalog author's credentials is optional but can establish the credibility of the writer. Each element has its own specific design and production guidelines to follow.

Depending on your personal preference, the size of a catalog can vary. Avoid producing a catalog that is oversized for your presentation package. Make a mock-up of your catalog using copies of your prints to get a feel for how the catalog will look when completed.

Mock-up Catalogs

It is important to develop a body of work that is consistent. Always think in terms of series and related works. We have provided a mock-up for you to use (see pages 217–240), when you consider publishing a catalog or documenting a select body of work. Follow the format provided or create your own mock-up on blank paper. After you have completed your mock-up catalog you can present it to printers for their bids.

I have found that by creating mock-up catalogs, artists are better able to see their work as a complete body of work, which helps them stay focused. For the images in the mock-up, just use snapshots of your works. If your photos of paintings include the frames, cut the frames out of the photos with an X-ACTO knife before you paste the photos on the page.

This catalog will consist of twelve sheets of paper including the cover. This is called a twenty-four page catalog. Do not clutter the pages with many images. Allow the work to be seen one at a time. In this case, less is more. Ideally, use one image for every two pages. If you decide you want to include more, I recommend not using more than one image per page for this catalog format.

If you do decide to print this catalog, I recommend using twelve point cover stock for the cover and ten-point book for the interior pages.

The catalog will consist of the following items:

1. Cover—always select your strongest image for the cover (impact is important)
2. Title Page—artist's name, name of exhibition or series of work, if you choose, or both
3. Essay—find a writer or begin to create your own story with a focus that a writer can follow. *Do not write your own essay for a printed catalog.* Fill out the writer's questionnaire. This will help you as well as your writer.
4. Artist statement—keep it short and to the point.
5. Biography
6. Title of work
7. Medium
8. Size
9. Date completed
10. Credit information

The Cover

The front cover of the presentation package is composed of an image and your name. The cover is the first impression a person may have of your work; therefore, the image you select needs to be of your strongest work. The goal of a strong cover is to grab the attention of the people you are presenting to so they look further at your works.

Because art images reproduced in print are taken more seriously, a catalog or brochure will add to your credibility. The catalog or brochure in your presentation must be clean and in excellent condition. Again, the first impression that your catalog or brochure creates can have such a positive impact that the piece may be the difference between success and failure.

Despite this importance, if you have the opportunity to present your work prior to finishing your catalog, by all means make the presentation. Let the recipient know that a catalog will be available shortly. Design your presentation as if you had a catalog. Use from nine to twenty images. Complete the catalog, folder presentation, or brochure as soon as possible (refer to the section on developing your presentation materials).

Images

The images reproduced in your catalog represent your strongest works. You have taken painstaking care to select the proper art pieces, to have quality photographs taken, to select the strongest image of each piece, and to print the photographs with the utmost clarity and contrast possible. The next step is to assemble these images into your catalog.

The image presented on the cover should be the strongest image in the catalog. Print the remaining images in the order in which each image is referenced in the academic essay. Images of art pieces specifically created in a series should be presented in the order in which the series was meant to be viewed.

The Academic Essay

The academic essay is an examination of the body of works being presented in your catalog. Often the essay compares your works to those of historical artists in style, medium, and message. The goal of an academic essay is to raise the credibility of your work within the art world and to create an understanding of your art in terms of contemporary and historical values.

Plan to hire a professional from the art community to write your essay: a college professor, an art dealer, a museum curator, or an art critic, for example. Select a person who is knowledgeable about your style of art and who has a strong understanding of art history in the context of your work. Interview each possible candidate make sure each likes your work and can see its place in the art world. You are asking your writer to attach his or her credibility to your essay so you want what is said to be positive but without undue hype.

The following is a brief excerpt from an essay written by Roberta Carasso, Ph.D. It is an excellent example of how an academic essay relates the artist's works to historical and social values.

Academic Essay Sample

CIVILIZED UNREST

The art of Myrella Moses can be linked to those nineteenth and twentieth century Western artists who recognized the value of Primitive art and incorporated its ideas into their creations. While having a similar affinity to the Primitive, a love and appreciation of the values it represents, Moses's art is not based on Primitive art, per se, but on the ideas Primitive art represents. Her art takes the Primitive legacy into the twenty-first century, where it becomes a focal point for humanity to reevaluate the substance of its life. Specifically, Moses's art confronts both the eradication of indigenous peoples from whose soul Primitive art emerges and the effects the eradication has on all humankind. Hence, the exhibition deals with the undercurrents of unrest smoldering in all civilized people, including the indigenous.

The ideas in this exhibition far exceed the making of art and are not limited to the aesthetics of Primitive art that captivated artists of the past. This art takes a broader view and looks at a phenomenon never considered by those who glorified the Primitive—that indigenous peoples are vanishing and could eventually become extinct. In this regard, Moses's concern for the essence of the Primitive returns the art to the very foundation the Primitive art makers had in mind—that art is a vehicle through which life's values are crystallized.

Primitive art extended significantly the known artistic vocabulary of the past two centuries. It yielded a far richer artistic palette that, directly or indirectly, affected many subsequent artistic movements, among them Cubism, Fauvism, German Expressionism, Surrealism, and even Futurism.

Artists such as Pablo Picasso, Andre Derain, Constantin Brancusi, and others were drawn to the Primitive, primarily the African aesthetic but also the arts of the South Pacific, South America, and Asia. They saw in the Primitive a freshness and simplicity, devoid of modernism and mechanization. The absence of individual artistic expression was innocent and unpretentious, yet, in its way, highly sophisticated in inventions and uses of form and space. The Primitive provided nineteenth and twentieth century artists with both a freer range of expression and a completely new turn to explore in the artistic road.

The Author's Biography

The author's biography is a brief statement about the writer's credentials within the art community. This statement demonstrates the credibility of the author and therefore lends to the credibility of your work. Including the author's biography in your catalog is optional and should be done only when the author's credentials are strong. Limit the author's biography to one or two paragraphs.

Writer's Questionnaire

You may also wish to fill out the writer's questionnaire and include it with your mock-up.

WRITER'S QUESTIONNAIRE FOR THE ARTIST

Treat each question as an interview from which your writer will get to know more about you and your art and in turn may select quotes to include in your essay. If you have any additional statements beyond the topics discussed below, feel free to include them.

Remember to provide slides and/or photographs of your works for the writer to view. Ideally, if you have selected the images that are to be used in your catalog, provide slides of those works, properly labeled with your name, the title of the image, media, dimensions, and year of creation. Indicate which image you have selected for the cover.

Date	*5/19/97*
Artist Name	*Robert Thomas*
Telephone	*(619) 555-8481*
Fax	*(619) 555-8492*
Internet	*are@artcommbech.com*

1. Are you a symbolic artist? Yes _*x*_ No ___

2. Where do you derive your symbols from?

   Religious subject matter and everyday life.

3. Who is your art for?

   The general public.

4. What is more important, the moment and act of creation, the message, or the material artwork?

   A combination; each plays an important role in my work, though the message is probably most important.

5. If you could not earn money through art, would you still be an artist?

   Yes. It is most important for me to express myself.

6. What is the role of the viewer relative to your artwork?

   Viewers are a very important part of the work as they provide me with an understanding of my art from a broader point of view than just my own.

7. What is the role of spontaneity and of control in your artwork?

   Very important, as I am an "action painter."

8. Discuss the elements of your artistic language.

   I want my art to communicate to the viewer through color and representational images.

9. What event most influenced your work and your choice to be an artist?

   A movie I saw on the life of Pablo Picasso.

10. What artists have had the greatest influence on your work?

    Bacom, Hocking, and Monet.

11. Is there a single, proper interpretation of your artwork?

    Expressionism.

12. Under what conditions would you refuse to sell or to have your works displayed?

    None.

13. What is unique about your work?

    The way the images seem to stick in people's minds. People tell me they remind them of their religious upbringing.

14. Is there a particular name you have for your style of art?

    Contemporary religious expressionism.

15. What is art, and how has it changed your life?

    Art is a total of expressionism and has allowed me to be free to express my ideas.

16. Is your art more personal, social, political, or nonobjective?

    My art is personal.

17. What is the role of emotion in the creation, the understanding, and the experience of your art?

My inspiration comes from emotional responses to events.

18. Is your art representational?

Yes __x__ No _____ In what sense?

I use figures and other representational subject matter.

19. Is your art abstract?

Yes __x__ No _____ In what sense?

It docs have some abstract aspect to it.

20. What are the unexplored frontiers for your art?

I'm still searching for those.

21. How important are the general public and the artistic community to your work?

I think its important to reach both. I would particularly like acceptance from the artist community.

22. How would you like for history to remember your art?

As an artist who had connection and commitment to my work.

23. Is there a medium you wish to explore?

    Film.

24. Why do you work in the medium that you do?

    It is easy and inexpensive for me.

Tear Sheets

A tear sheet (also referred to as an information sheet or flyer) is usually a single presentation sheet that includes a brief essay, one or two images of your work, and a selected listing of exhibitions. The tear sheet functions in place of or in addition to a catalog or brochure. In the absence of a catalog or brochure, a tear sheet still gives you the opportunity to express the importance of your work with supportive images. Always support the tear sheet with the remainder of your presentation package, including photographs, slides, and other materials.

The Artist's Biography

The artist's biography is a selected listing of all institutional and gallery exhibitions of your work. Information about your education, teaching experience, commissions, and the like is usually not included in a catalog or brochure. The catalog biography is only a portion of your complete résumé. List your exhibitions in chronological order, going back from two to five years. This list will demonstrate your recent activities as an artist. If you have important experiences further back in your career, such as having won a prestigious prize when you were young, by all means include those events in your biography.

Include in your biography all institutional events, gallery showings, juried competitions, and selected important benefit events. For the commercial artist, the biography will demonstrate that you are viewed by the art community as a viable commodity. Include the names of the institutions that have purchased your work for their collections. Private collectors are usually not listed in a biography unless the collector is someone of great importance to the art community. If you have only had a few exhibitions or collectors, do not worry. The essay will express the importance of your work.

The Professional Artist's Résumé or Curriculum Vitae

The artist's résumé is a complete synopsis of exhibition experience, grants and awards, professional experience, education, collectors, editorials, and publications. The purpose of the résumé is to give the reader a full understanding of your involvement and accomplishments within the art world. The résumé will be used to supplement the selected biography within your printed presentation materials.

An artist's résumé must be written clearly and concisely, and printed in an easy-to-read format. The content of your résumé tells a story of your accomplishments within the art world. The first element is a brief biographical statement including your place and date of birth and a synopsis of your development as an artist. This statement is written in the same tone as the academic essay and includes references to important artists or professionals with whom you have studied or worked, or who have influenced you. All this information should be stated in no more than two brief paragraphs.

List your exhibitions in reverse chronological order, with the current year listed first. The list should go back for the previous two to five years. This list will demonstrate your current activities as a professional artist. Include all institutional events, gallery showings, juried competitions, and selected important benefit events.

Format each entry beginning with the year of the event, title of the exhibition, name of the institution or gallery holding the event, and the city, state, and country location of the event. For events occurring in the same year, list the year once and let the format of the page show the remaining entries occurred in the same year. For example:

1997	*A Room with a View*	*A Woman of Strength*
	Modern Museum of Art	The Woman's Contemporary Museum
	Santa Ana, CA, USA	Los Angeles, CA, USA

Present the information in as academic a fashion as possible. Give the name of a location correctly but make it as academic sounding as possible. One-person shows that did not have a specific title may be listed under your name. Above all else, be honest with what you say in your biography. You can count on the fact that anyone seriously considering showing your work will check you out thoroughly.

Depending on your preference, you may list solo exhibitions separately from group exhibitions. My preference is to do so if the artist has had a fair number of solo shows. If the artist has had primarily group events, I would group these together. When solo shows are listed separately, use the heading "Selected Solo Exhibitions." In turn, title the group exhibitions "Selected Group Exhibitions." List all solo shows in chronological order before starting a new section for group exhibitions.

The next element is to show the reader that the art community has recognized the importance of your work through the various awards, honors, and grants you have received. List these entries in precisely the same format as an exhibition entry, for example:

1997	Randall Francis Community Grant
	The Randall Francis Foundation
	Los Angeles, CA, USA

A list of the important collections that hold your work is an important element of your résumé. Include all personal, corporate, and institutional collections. If your works are collected by someone who is respected within the art world, others will perceive your work as worthy.

***EXAMPLE:* ARTIST'S RESUME**

CARMEN STAVROS

Born: 1953, Scottsdale, Arizona.

Stavros studied Fine Arts at Arizona State University and the Art Institute of Southern California. She also studied with Roger Armestead, Sam Clayburn, George Galliger, Tom Gallant, Robert Wing, and Milford Zin. Stavros has her bachelor's and master's degrees in fine arts. She is known in the Southwestern art community for her strong compositions and her vibrant use of color.

Recent Solo Exhibitions

1997 *Carmen Stavros*
Harthbrook Museum
Scottsdale, AZ, USA

1996 *Sticks and Stones*
Gavin Smith Gallery
Los Angeles, CA, USA

1996 *A Woman in Motion*
South Bay Gallery
Pasadena, CA, USA

1995 *Stick Figures*
Art in Space Museum
New York, NY, USA

1995 *Glass Houses*
Art in Space Museum
New York, NY, USA

1994 *She Sez*
Cantorland Gallery
Chicago, IL, USA

Recent Group Exhibitions

1997 *Currents*
Time Stop Gallery
Scottsdale, AZ, USA

1997 *Tide Watch*
Southern Artists Museum
Scottsdale, AZ, USA

1996 *Stavros, Smith & Watson*
Southern Artists Museum
Scottsdale, AZ, USA

1996 *Women in Motion*
South Bay Gallery
Pasadena, CA, USA

1995 *Still Life—After Life*
Art in Space Museum
New York, NY, USA

1995 *Woman Media*
Gavin Smith Gallery
Los Angeles, CA, USA

1995 *Currents*
Time Space Gallery
Laguna Beach, CA, USA

1994 *Sacred Signals*
Grace Main Gallery
New York, NY, USA

Awards and Honors

1995 *Randall Francis Community Grant*
The Randall Francis Foundation
Los Angeles, CA, USA

1995 Female Artist of the Year
Southern States Artist Guild
Los Angeles, CA, USA

Selected Collections

State University Fine Arts Museum
Imperial University
English Council of Fine Arts
Cleveland Museum of Contemporary Arts
The Hopkins Estate

Professional Experience

1997 *Sculpture with Wood.* Lecture series at California College of the Arts, Los Angeles, CA.

Education

1971–74 Bachelor of Fine Arts, Arizona State University.

1974–77 Master of Fine Arts, Art Institute of Southern California.

Publications

Anderson, Julian. *The Strength of Women in Art.* Catalog. The Southern States Artist Guild, October 30–December 9, 1995.

Beckton, William. *Carmen Stavros—A Woman In Motion.* Catalog. The Southern States Art Guild, January 15–February 10, 1996.

Feather, Anthony. Putting Down Foundations, *Feminist Art World,* 3, no. 6 (December 1992), 35.

Stavros, Carmen. *Sticks and Stones.* Catalog. Gavin Smith Gallery, February 15–March 1, 1996.

Thomas, Anthony. Glass Houses, *Arts Institutional,* 6, no. 2 (February 1995).

Wiggins, Daniel. *Currents.* Catalog. Time Space Gallery, August 15–September 1, 1995.

Selected Collections

Listing the important collections of your work is an important element to your résumé. Include personal, corporate, and institutional collections in your résumé. If your works are collected by someone who is respected within the art world, your work is perceived to be worthy of the level of importance of these collections. List the collections by the collection names and not by the collector's names, unless the collections are commonly referred to by name. Collection entries are formatted with the name of the collection and the city, state, and country of their location. For example, the Brunheiber Collection is located in New York. The entry would read:

> The Brunheiber Collection
> New York, NY, USA

The element of the résumé that describes your professional experience is important. It tells the reader about your background above and beyond the exhibitions you have had. The professional experience relates to those things you have done and accomplished as a professional artist, such as lectures you may have given, teaching you may have provided to artists, and participation in artist-in-residence programs.

The importance of education has been reflected throughout this book. It is your key to understanding the historical and contemporary influences of the art around you. It will help you to understand your own place within the art world. Do not be concerned if your education is limited, although in some cases an extensive education can be helpful. The important component of your career is for your work to be strong. List the formal education you do have as well as the artists with whom you have studied.

It is also important to list catalogs and publications that show your work. Again, you are establishing the importance of your art to the reader. Any magazines, books, or news articles that discussed your work should also be included. This information is listed in a format similar to that you would find in a bibliography for a research paper. Always include the author's name with the title of the publication.

Presentation Binder

The presentation binder is a great way to get started if you are in a hurry or on a budget. This binder should be white, about one-half inch thick, with a clear plastic pocket on the cover, allowing you to insert an image of your work. Your binder will also contain an essay relating to your work, your artist's statement, your biography, at least three 8" × 10" color photos and one or two 8" × 10" black-and-white photos and between nine and twenty properly labeled slides. If you are presenting to a gallery, art publisher, or potential client, you may also include a price list. Do not send a price list to a museum or similar institution. Optional items to include in the binder are press releases and other promotional materials. All items in the binder should be inserted in clear plastic pocket pages.

Photographic Prints

Following the catalog or brochure are the three color 8" × 10" prints. If you are not providing a catalog, the prints should follow the cover letter. After the color prints, enclose the properly labeled one or two 8" × 10" black-and-white prints. Use the same label format as that for the color prints.

Every print or slide enclosed in your presentation packages must be properly labeled. Never send out an image that is not properly identified. Each print should be labeled on the center of its reverse side. Again, handwritten labels are not acceptable. Typed labels are adequate, but laser-printed labels are better.

Labels for laser printers are available at office supplies stores. A good label size for prints is a 1" × 2-5/8." At the most, the label will have five lines, as follows:

1. Artist's name
2. Name of piece
3. Media used
4. Dimensions of piece
5. Year piece was created (optional)

In designating the dimensions of a painting, state height by width; for a sculpture, state height by width by depth. For an art piece that does not have a title, use the phrase "Untitled" on the second line.

Slides

Following the black-and-white prints are 35 mm color slides. The slides should be in a clear plastic slide sheet in the same order as the images appear in the catalog. Use only slide sheets that hold the exact number of slides you are presenting. For example, use a nine-pocket slide sheet when presenting nine images. Never use a slide sheet with empty pockets because the unfilled spaces suggest something is missing from your presentation.

Identify each slide with a laser-printed label. The format for the slide label is identical to that for the print, but the label is smaller. I use a laser label that is 1/2" × 1-3/4." The type size must be small—about 6-point type.

Apply the label to the slide pocket position. Position the label on the pocket so that it is across the bottom front of the slide. If a slide must be viewed on its side, purchase small press-on arrows and apply an arrow pointing to the correct slide positioning.

Press and Promotional Materials

The next element is not required for a presentation package but can be beneficial. This element includes press releases and promotional materials. If you include such materials in your presentation, use only those that are compatible with the type of venue you are soliciting. Send a gallery the press release from a gallery or a museum; send a museum materials related to academic events. When sending to galleries, you may also include promotion-oriented materials, invitations, and articles from newspapers, magazines, and other sources.

Self-addressed, Stamped Envelope

The final piece of the package is not related to your artwork but shows consideration to the recipient. Enclose a self-addressed, stamped envelope for returning your presentation materials. If you do not enclose one, you may never get the package back. Your presentation package is difficult and costly to put together. You want to do everything possible to make sure your materials are returned so you can reuse them.

PRESENTATION CHECKLIST SUMMARY REVIEW

Cover Letter

The presentation cover letter is designed to introduce you and your art to the prospective venue.

> **QUICK TIP**
>
> Make sure you select your strongest work.

Catalog, Brochure, or Biography Page

The purpose of the catalog is to elevate your image as an artist and the importance of your work in the art world. It can be a four-page brochure or a nine- to twenty-image catalog, comprising twenty-four or more pages. If your budget does not allow for either, use a biographical sheet. As soon as you can, augment the sheet with a brochure, catalog, and presentation binder. It's important to have printed materials in your presentation.

Photographic Prints (color and black and white)

Color prints support the other components of your presentation package by showing the detail of a few select pieces. The 8" × 10" black-and-white prints demonstrate your readiness to promote your work because newspapers prefer this format.

Color Slides

The color slides should support each image printed in your catalog or brochure. Use slide sheets that match the number of images in your printed materials. Never present a package where empty spaces exist in the slide sheet.

Padded Mailing Envelope and Self-addressed, Stamped Return Envelope

The padded mailing envelope with cardboard inserts will protect your presentation package. The self-addressed, stamped return envelope is enclosed for the return of your package after it has been reviewed.

Press Packet (optional)

A press packet shows that your work has been exhibited in the community. The prospective venue will note responses you received in prior exhibitions, which can make exhibiting your work desirable. For example, a museum invitation is especially attractive to a gallery and gives you a great deal of credibility. You can also include photocopies of positive reviews of your work from newspapers and magazines.

EXAMPLE: PRESENTATION CHECKLIST

- _x_ Cover letter
- _x_ Essay and artist's statement (optional)
- _x_ Catalog, brochure, biography page, presentation binder, CD-ROM, etc.
- _x_ Three 8" × 10" or 8-1/2" × 11" color photographs
- _x_ One or two 8" × 10" or 8-1/2" × 11" black-and-white photographs
- _x_ Nine to twenty properly labeled slides of all pieces shown in the catalog or brochure
- _x_ Press releases and promotional materials ready for print (optional). A price list (only if sending to galleries).
- _x_ Self-addressed, stamped padded envelope for return of presentation materials

Remaining Archive Materials

- _x_ An up-to-date academic résumé (updated throughout your career)
- _x_ Letters received from dealers, curators, and others discussing your works (positive or negative)
- _x_ Black-and-white installation photographs
- _x_ Photographs of important people attending your show
- _x_ Invitations to shows/exhibitions
- _x_ Press releases regarding shows/exhibitions
- _x_ All promotional materials for each show/exhibition
- _x_ Newspaper reviews of your works/shows/exhibitions (positive or negative)
- _x_ Magazine reviews of your works/shows/exhibitions
- _x_ Brochures, tear sheets, etc.
- _x_ Other materials about you or your works from the art community

EXAMPLE: COVER LETTER

Ms. Michelle Talvison
1556 South Watkins Drive
Los Angeles, CA 90046
(213) 555-1212

January 1, 1997

Ms. Catherine Kingston
Curator
The Contemporary Museum
5504 Broad Street
Los Angeles, CA 90046

Dear Catherine:

It was a pleasure speaking with you this morning. As I mentioned, Robert Gaffey, a board member of your museum, suggested I contact you. After personally visiting my exhibition at the Rothkeller Institute, he felt the style, media, and subject matter of my work ties directly into the focus of your museum.

My work has been widely exhibited on the West Coast and Pacific Rim, including the Mockteller Museum in San Francisco, the Alternative Museum in Los Angeles, and the Modern Museum in San Diego. The intensity of my paintings has been compared to that of Richter, Michaels, and Bellington. Each piece addresses issues confronting society today.

Catherine, I have enclosed presentation materials for your review, including a catalog from my current show at the Blumschmelt Gallery. I will call you again next week to discuss your response to my work and your interest in the possibility of an exhibition.

Sincerely,

Michelle Talvison

Encl. Presentation Materials

EXAMPLE: BIOGRAPHY SHEETS

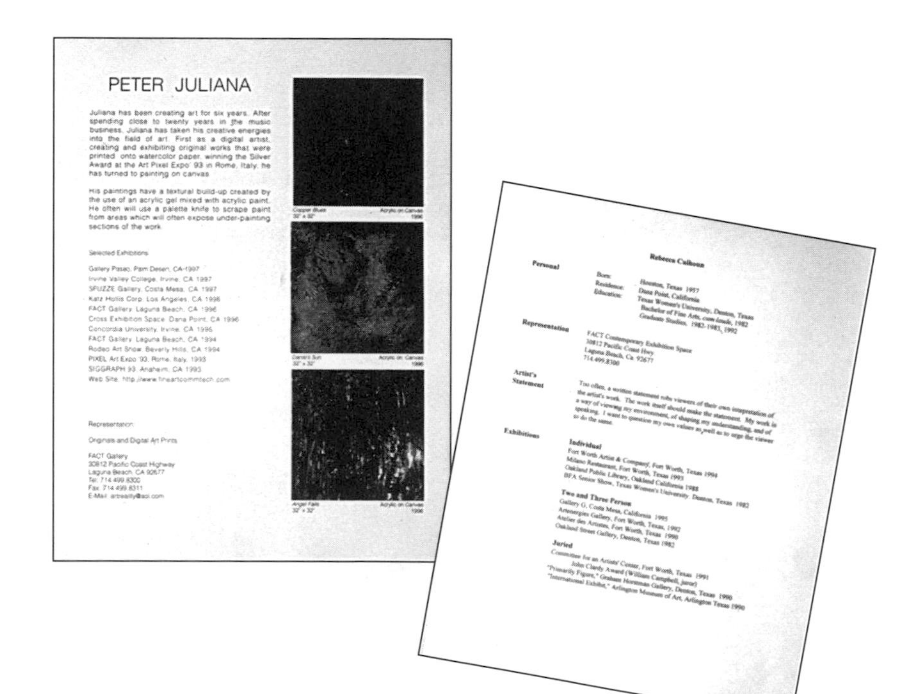

PETER JULIANA

Juliana has been creating art for six years. After spending close to twenty years in the music business, Juliana has taken his creative energies into the field of art. First as a digital artist, creating and exhibiting original works that were printed onto watercolor paper, winning the Silver Award at the Art Pixel Expo' 93 in Rome, Italy, he has turned to painting on canvas.

His paintings have a textural build-up created by the use of an acrylic gel mixed with acrylic paint. He often will use a palette knife to scrape paint from areas which will often expose under-painting sections of the work.

Selected Exhibitions

Gallery Paseo, Palm Desert, CA 1997
Irvine Valley College, Irvine, CA 1997
SPUZZE Gallery, Costa Mesa, CA 1997
Katz Hollis Corp. Los Angeles, CA 1996
FACT Gallery, Laguna Beach, CA 1996
Cross Exhibition Space, Dana Point, CA 1996
Concordia University, Irvine, CA 1995
FACT Gallery, Laguna Beach, CA 1994
Rodeo Art Show, Beverly Hills, CA 1994
PIXEL Art Expo '93, Rome, Italy 1993
SIGGRAPH 93, Anaheim, CA 1993
Web Site: http://www.fineartcommtech.com

Representation:

Originals and Digital Art Prints

FACT Gallery
30812 Pacific Coast Highway
Laguna Beach, CA 92677
Tel: 714 499 8300
Fax: 714 499 8311
E-Mail: artreality@aol.com

Rebecca Calhoun

Personal
Born: Houston, Texas 1957
Residence: Dana Point, California
Education: Texas Woman's University, Denton, Texas
Bachelor of Fine Arts, cum laude, 1982
Graduate Studies, 1982-1983, 1992

Representation
FACT Contemporary Exhibition Space
30812 Pacific Coast Hwy
Laguna Beach, Ca. 92677
714.499.8300

Artist's Statement
Too often, a written statement robs viewers of their own interpretation of the artist's work. The work itself should make the statement. My work is a way of viewing my environment, of shaping my understanding, and of speaking. I want to question my own values as well as to urge the viewer to do the same.

Exhibitions

Individual
Fort Worth Artist & Company, Fort Worth, Texas 1994
Milano Restaurant, Fort Worth, Texas 1993
Oakland Public Library, Oakland California 1988
BFA Senior Show, Texas Women's University, Denton, Texas 1982

Two and Three Person
Gallery G, Costa Mesa, California 1995
Artenergies Gallery, Fort Worth, Texas, 1992
Atelier des Artistes, Fort Worth, Texas 1990
Oakland Street Gallery, Denton, Texas 1982

Juried
Committee for an Artists' Center, Fort Worth, Texas 1991
John Clardy Award (William Campbell, juror)
"Primarily Figure," Graham Horstman Gallery, Denton, Texas 1990
"International Exhibit," Arlington Museum of Art, Arlington Texas 1990

EXAMPLE: **TWO BLACK-AND-WHITE PHOTOS (8" × 10")**
THREE COLOR PHOTOS (8" × 10")
PROPER LABELING

EXAMPLE: **SLIDES**

Always send complete slide sheets and labeled properly.

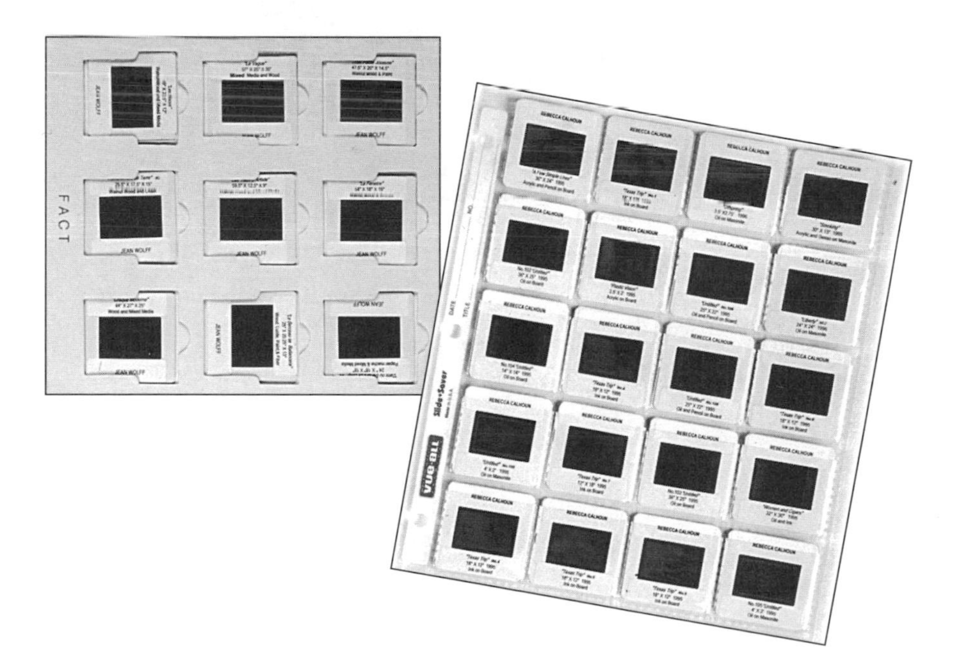

***EXAMPLE:* TEAR SHEETS**

EXAMPLE: BROCHURE

Select a strong visual image for the cover.

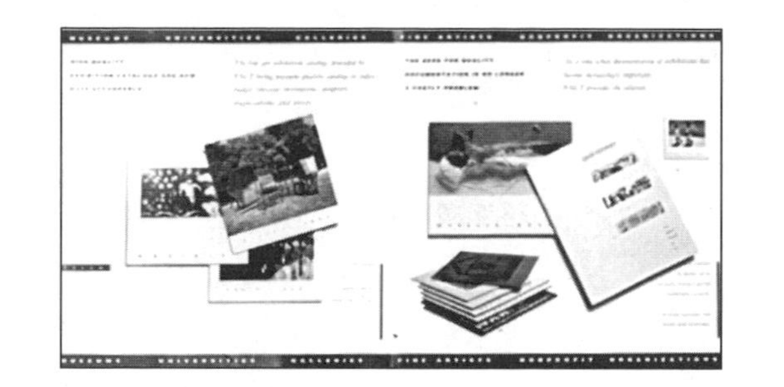

EXAMPLE: BINDER PACKAGE

You can create a great presentation using a view binder, color copy and a bit of work.

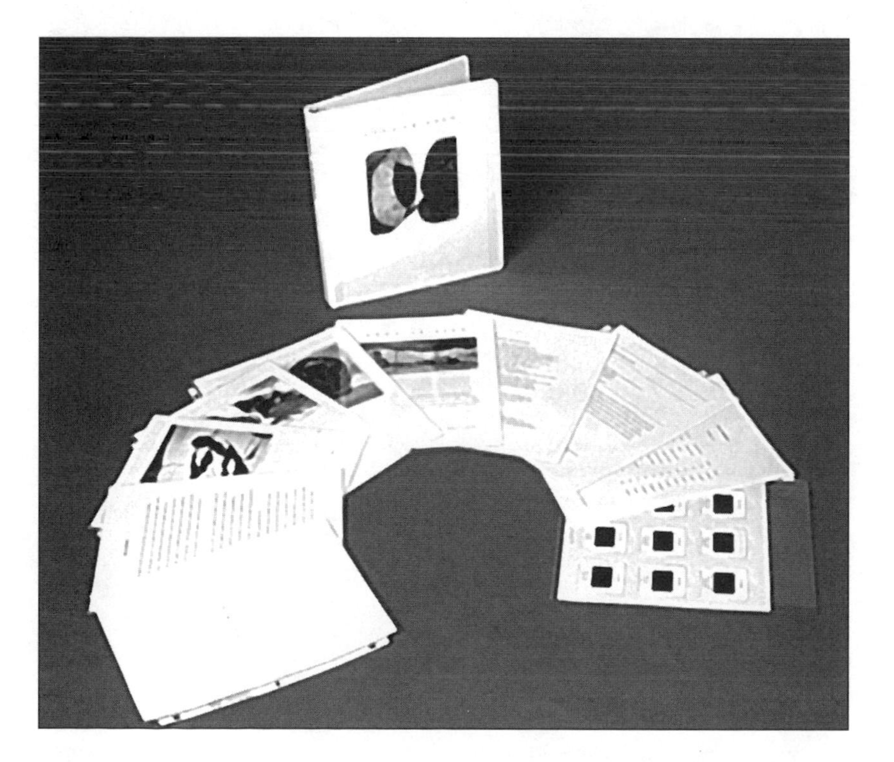

***EXAMPLE:* CATALOGS**

Perfect binding allows the artist's name to be viewed on a shelf. This also allows the catalog to be referenced in catalog libraries.

***EXAMPLE:* CATALOGS**

The cover is important. Select a strong image that will interest people to open and look past the front cover.

EXAMPLE: **PADDED ENVELOPE AND SELF-ADDRESSED RETURN ENVELOPE**

EXAMPLE: **PRESS RELEASE LABELED PRESS PHOTO NEWSPAPER REVIEW**

EXAMPLE: **VIDEO & CD**

EXAMPLE: COMPLETE PRESENTATION

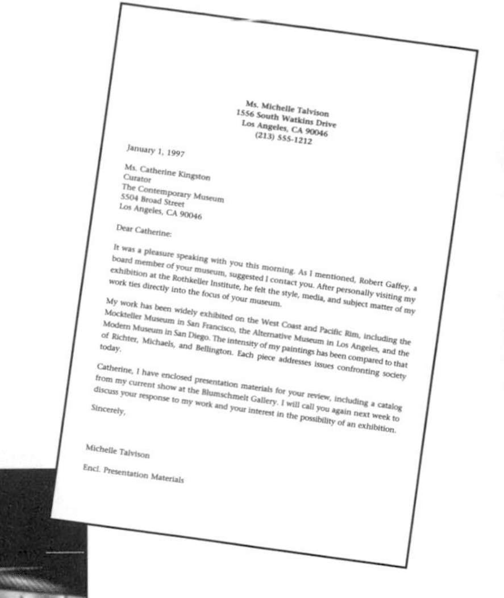

Ms. Michelle Talvison
1556 South Watkins Drive
Los Angeles, CA 90046
(213) 555-1212

January 1, 1997

Ms. Catherine Kingston
Curator
The Contemporary Museum
5504 Broad Street
Los Angeles, CA 90046

Dear Catherine:

It was a pleasure speaking with you this morning. As I mentioned, Robert Gaffey, a board member of your museum, suggested I contact you. After personally visiting my exhibition at the Rothkeller Institute, he felt the style, media, and subject matter of my work ties directly into the focus of your museum.

My work has been widely exhibited on the West Coast and Pacific Rim, including the Mockteller Museum in San Francisco, the Alternative Museum in Los Angeles, and the Modern Museum in San Diego. The intensity of my paintings has been compared to that of Richter, Michaels, and Bellington. Each piece addresses issues confronting society today.

Catherine, I have enclosed presentation materials for your review, including a catalog from my current show at the Blumschmelt Gallery. I will call you again next week to discuss your response to my work and your interest in the possibility of an exhibition.

Sincerely,

Michelle Talvison

Encl. Presentation Materials

The complete presentation consists of the following:

- Cover letter
- Catalog, brochure, or tear sheet
- Three color photos
- Two black-and-white photos
- Slides (labeled)
- Current biography
- Self-addressed stamped envelope

Sequence in order of placement. This doesn't mean you cannot present unless you have all of the above, but this should be a goal.

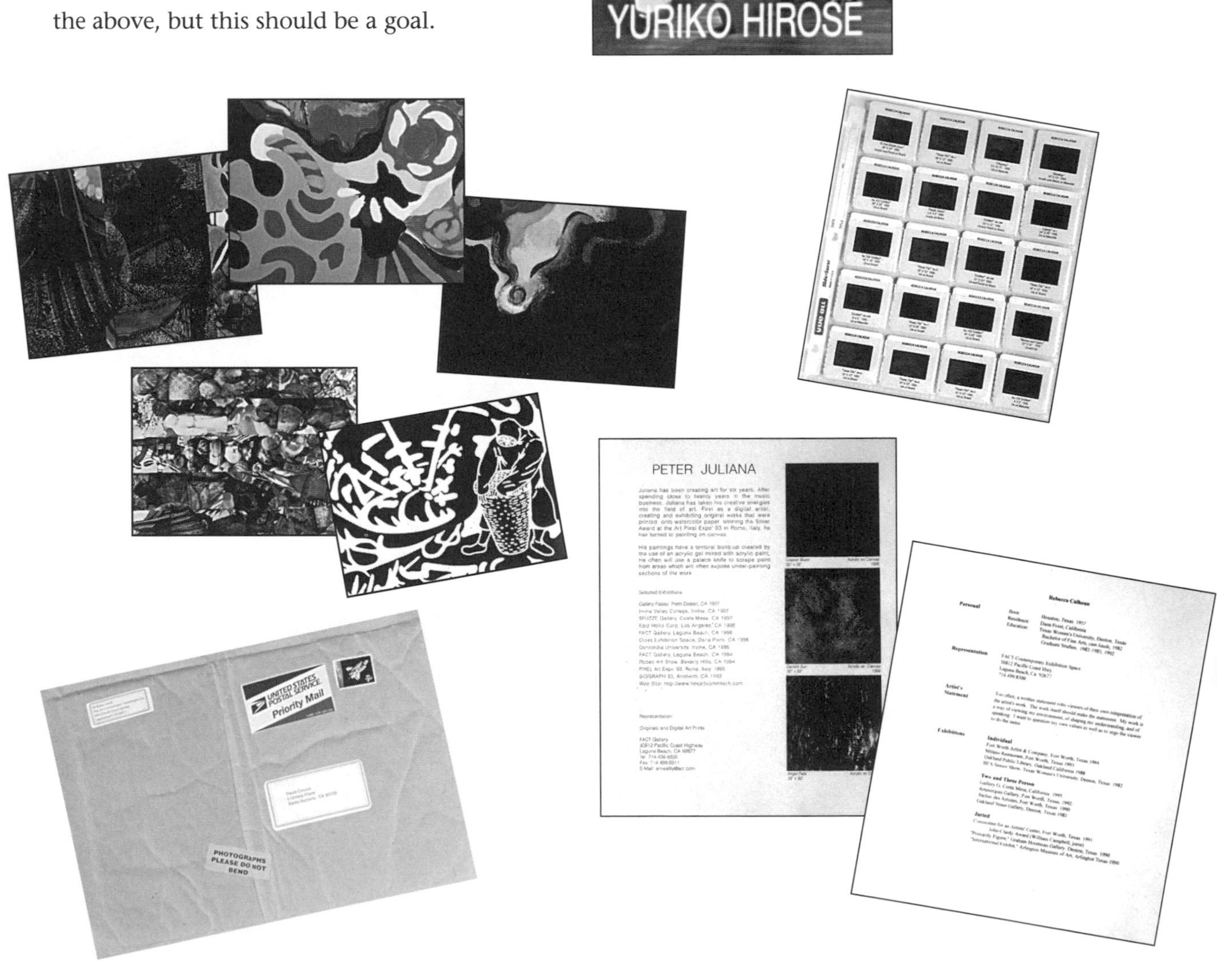

THE ARCHIVE

The master archive is a complete history of your career. It consists of your presentation materials, résumés, promotional materials, invitations, newspaper and magazine reviews, referral letters, slides, transparencies, and photographs.

QUICK TIP

Keep records of everything related to your art career.

Although developing an archive is a simple process, it does require an effort to keep track of what is published about you. When a new piece is photographed, a newspaper review (good or bad) comes out, or an invitation for a show is printed, immediately add it to your archive. Always try to obtain copies of each piece. The archive is a chronology of your development as an artist.

Most of the materials in the archive are under your control. For example, the invitations, press releases, promotional materials, referral letters, photographs, and slides are either initiated by you or by gallery or museum contacts whose activities you will know of. The only materials requiring diligence to locate are the printed reviews of your work in newspapers or magazines.

If you do not have time to track newspaper and magazine stories, clipping services can do this for you. These services track your name through a variety of newspapers and magazines and then provide a copy of each article they find. Fees vary widely depending on the level of research you wish. You can contact an advertising agency for referrals to clipping services.

The Binder

Assemble your archive in a three-ring binder. The cover should have a clear pocket on the cover. Insert an 8 1/2" x 11" black-and-white reproduction of your work in the cover.

All archive materials should be inserted into clear plastic pocket pages. The pages allow you to remove items easily during an interview without repeatedly opening and closing the binder rings. The plastic pages also keep smaller items, such as invitations, neatly together, and you won't damage larger items with a three-hole punch.

Organizing the Archive

The first section of the archive is the master of your current presentation package. Insert the materials in the same order as in the presentation binder. As you update your presentation package with a new catalog or brochure and with new prints and slides, keep this section of your archive current. Your older presentation packages should be behind the master of your current package. The older packages are a quick reference about your development as an artist. It is important to keep up-to-date on your archive materials. For example, people who write about you today are also working to build their own careers. In a few years, they may become important art writers. What they said about you in the past will take on an even greater significance.

Academic Résumé

The artist's academic résumé is a complete listing of exhibitions, education, teaching experience, and any other pertinent information demonstrating your development as an artist. Think of the artist's résumé as being the art community's version of an employment résumé. The first item in the résumé will be the description of yourself as an artist that you created in the chapter, "Describing Your Art—Who are You?" but edited to read in the third person. Make five copies of your current résumé. Résumé writing rules and examples are provided in the chapter, "Written Communications."

Letters Received from Dealers, Curators, and Others

Letters received from dealers, curators, collectors, people who have influenced your art, and critics are very powerful testimonials to the importance of your work to the art community. Keep all incoming and outgoing communications on file.

Installation Photographs

Installation photographs transport the viewer from imagining your works displayed to actually seeing them hung. If you produce larger works the photographs allow for a better presentation. Establish a photographic file of shows and locations where your works have been exhibited. Include photographs that show people viewing your work.

Photographs of Important People Attending Your Show

Your art will receive increased credibility and value by virtue of the company it keeps, both the artists who exhibit alongside your work and those who come to see it. If a respected individual from the art community makes the effort to view your works, there must be an interest. Others in the art community will be sensitive to who attends your shows.

Act as your own "paparazzi." When a person of importance attends one of your art functions, graciously introduce yourself. Prearrange for someone to take photographs of the two of you conversing. Don't forget to listen to what the person has to say about your work. Meetings like these underscore why it is so important for you to appear at all events associated with the exhibition of your works. A successful artist will network. You never know who may be involved with any given venue and who could be a good contact for your career.

Remaining Materials

Finally, your archive should include all the remaining materials you collect from each event in which you participate. These include invitations, press releases, promotional materials, newspaper and magazine reviews (positive and negative), brochures, tear sheets, and any other materials pertaining to you or your works. When possible, collect multiple copies of each piece.

6 TARGETING PROSPECTIVE VENUES

You may be a professional artist with years of education and experience or a part-time artist ready to make a first attempt at getting gallery representation. Regardless of your status, gallery representation is your opportunity to present your art to the public and the art world. So do not underestimate the importance of doing your homework and planning your actions. Aside from your talent and preparedness of presentation materials, your knowledge regarding each venue will put you on the right track.

QUICK TIP

Be knowledgeable about the venue you are approaching for representation.

The goal of qualifying targets is to find galleries, museums, and other venues that are most likely to exhibit your works. The key is to learn as much as you possibly can about each marketplace.

You can obtain information, news, services, and contacts from numerous sources. I strongly recommend that you join an arts organization. These organizations provide excellent information about what is happening in your area, resources you can contact for services, discounts provided to the organization's members, and so forth. Many arts organizations provide programs for further education and promotion of their member artists.

Also subscribe to art publications or review them in the library. Select a few national or international publications, but don't overlook local and regional magazines. Your career plan may focus on international exhibitions, but you must first walk before you run. So keep abreast of local and regional events.

Read reviews of exhibitions in your area. Art critics keep on top of who and what is happening in the local art community. Also attend exhibitions for education, information, and establishing contacts. When you go to exhibitions, talk with other artists.

Qualifying your prospective venues will be most successful when you approach them in an organized, step-by-step fashion. As you learn about venues, doors will begin to open for you. You will be able to weed out venues that are not of interest and focus your effort on key targets. No matter what your objective—representation, exhibition, or funding—it is imperative that you know as much as possible about your target before presenting your work.

Create a List of Prospective Venues

The first step is to list the venues in your marketplace. Many reference books and magazines list galleries, museums, and institutions with a synopsis of current information about each. Check your public or university libraries, bookstores, and art supply stores for these publications. Also, a number of industry magazines publish yearly guides to the marketplace that are sold on newsstands and in large bookstores.

You will be inundated with names and places to research. Do not overwhelm yourself with an enormous list of candidates. Make two lists: an "A" list of venues of greatest interest and a "B" list of possible venues. Bypass those that do not seem to apply to you. The result will be a streamlined list of venues to which you will present your materials.

Expand Existing Opportunities

If you already have dealer representation but would like to expand your market, ask your dealer to help you in contacting galleries in new areas. Although most dealers rarely promote an artist beyond their geographical region, most dealers have associates outside the community. To make this proposition attractive, prepare all the materials yourself and offer the dealer a percentage of your profits from the resulting outside sales. Most dealers will work harder for you if they know they will be compensated. The added visibility of your work will be worth the expense.

Call for Information

The next step in finding prospective venues is to telephone each one on your list to gather basic information. I call this process "telephone research" and telephone research questionnaires have been provided in this book for you to use. There are specific questions you will ask a gallery, museum, or institution before you present in person or by mail.

QUICK TIP

Keep your mind open for opportunities.

For each venue you call, complete a research sheet by recording all the information you learn about that venue. These sheets become part of your career plan materials. It is imperative you be prepared for that unexpected moment when an important contact presents itself.

Just such an opportunity for me arose out of the blue. An artist friend asked me to contact a gallery in New York on his behalf. I called the gallery and struck up a lengthy conversation with the director. We built a nice rapport over the phone. During the conversation she realized I was an artist as well. She asked me to send information about my art. As soon as we finished our conversation, I express mailed one of my presentation packages to her. It arrived in New York the next morning.

I received a call the same day. The director said she was very impressed with my presentation. In all her years as a dealer, she added, she had never had an artist respond so quickly and professionally to a request for information. An exhibition was booked and an agreement transmitted to me the same day. (By the way, my artist friend was also included in an exhibition with this gallery.)

Always have your materials in order and ready to be mailed or you will undoubtedly lose out on unexpected opportunities. If you are serious about having your work exhibited, there is no excuse for not having a professional presentation package. I often hear artists say, "I'm not quite ready yet." One artist recently told me she had sold over 70 pieces during a summer art show. She wants gallery representation, but doesn't feel quite ready. She already knows she has work that sells well, and all that's required is for her to develop a professional presentation package so she can successfully approach the venues in which she wants exposure.

When to Call

Timing is important when creating opportunities for yourself. There are good and bad days to call a venue for information. With a little thought, you can generally figure out which days those are.

Many venues are closed Sundays and Mondays. Use these days for doing something else in your career plan. Saturdays are busy days for galleries, museums, and other venues as well as for their decision makers. Keep in mind that your goal is to speak directly to the person who makes the decisions.

Tuesday, Wednesday, and Thursday are the best days to call since you are most likely to reach the decision maker on those days. This is not to say that you must only call on these three days. But it's probably best to make your introductory calls on one of those days. If you are told to call back on another day, put it in your calendar and do so. You have now started the ball rolling.

Number of Venues to Call

Call only as many venues as you can follow up on promptly. If you communicate with a venue and do not respond in a timely fashion, you will create the impression that you are not serious, not organized, or possibly not easy to work with. Continue to make calls until you find a contact that expresses interest in seeing your work. Follow up the same day, using the methods in the chapter "Presenting Your Work." Once you have exhausted the possibility of working with this venue, continue your research until you find another active venue.

Do not present to too many venues at one time. Word will get around that you are canvassing the area. Be selective about the venues you choose to approach. You want to work with the best venues.

Referrals and Rapport

Besides obtaining information, you want to build a rapport with the venue decision maker. If you were referred by an influential person, mention that person within your opening statement. Ask for the name of the person who answers and the address the person by name. Speak clearly and in a strong, confident tone. The purpose of this initial telephone call is to create a favorable first impression and gather useful information.

Thank You Is Always Appropriate

Be friendly and professional on the phone. Thank the person for his or her time. A considerate and appreciative manner, regardless of whether the person has been helpful, can ensure that doors will remain open to you.

Sample Conversation—A Scripted Guide

Some people are not comfortable with soliciting information by phone. Don't be concerned. I assure you, you are not alone. I have "scripted" some opening lines that may be helpful. Create a script that reflects your personality. Remember, be professional.

Good morning (afternoon, evening)

Hello, my name is ______________________*. To whom am I speaking, please?*

Hi, ____________________________.

I was referred to you by ________________________ *(name of the referring party).*

I would like to ask you about your ______________________ *(venue type).*

—or—

Could you tell me about your ________________________ *(venue type)?*

QUICK TIP

It's important to be friendly.

If the person on the phone is agreeable to answering questions, ask for information that goes beyond the basic data you already obtained from the reference publications. Ask questions that are specific to the venue. You want information that is important to you. If the person is not available for questioning, ask to set a time for a phone appointment or, better yet, an appointment for a personal presentation. Some sample questions include the following: Are you accepting new artists to your gallery? How often do you accept new artists? What are the criteria for accepting new artists?

If you feel you are not ready to call strangers, you may ask a friend to do your calling. Select someone who is an extrovert. A second party can expound on your good points without sounding boastful. Remember to educate that person thoroughly on your work. Run through the presentation until your spokesperson knows it perfectly.

Get Started

Now that you have the ground rules, it is time to start carrying out plan—the biggest step in forging a successful career.

Once you have established relationships with a number of venues, you should become busy. But continue researching and contacting venues, even if only for a few hours a week. It is important to keep your "feelers" out. One of your venues may fall by the wayside and you will need to find a replacement.Venue research is an ongoing process. Do not stop. If you have someone who can help you stay organized and keep the process going, work with that person to actively research new opportunities. Keep on presenting.

Telephone Research Worksheets

The following questions and worksheets will help you gather important information about the galleries, museums, dealers, and other venues you are interested in pursuing. Some of the information can be obtained in books and magazines; other information you will gather through phone conversations. As you learn more, note it on the worksheet.

It is important for you to maintain a worksheet for each venue, even for those venues from which you receive negative responses. Future opportunity to work with that venue may arise, and it's important for you to have a record of prior contacts.

Make a number of copies of each type of worksheet for your research files. Keep a separate sheet for each targeted venue.

Telephone Research

When researching galleries, museums, publishers, and other organizations, you should obtain a great amount of detailed information. This information will be most valuable when you evaluate whether the venue is suitable for you and your art. Besides data on the Telephone Research Worksheet, you should also seek other pertinent information as indicated below.

Galleries, Independent Dealers, and Other Venues

What are the venue's hours?

What type of venue is it? Fine art gallery, co-op, commercial gallery, gallery chain, other?

What types of art are exhibited in this place?

What is the focus of the venue?

Does the venue handle originals, limited editions, prints, secondary product lines (T-shirts, etc.)?

How large is the space?

What are the ceiling heights?

What is the price range of art sold?

What artists does the venue currently represent?

Does the venue take on new artists?

What are the presentation policies?

To whom should materials be directed?

How long has the venue been in business?

How often does the venue have openings?

What types of shows are featured? Solo? Group? Other?

What kinds of promotions are done for each show? (Receptions, invitations, brochures, press releases, catalogs, flyers, advertisement, tear sheets, posters?)

If the venue has funds budgeted for the promotional materials, will the venue contribute to the expenses?

Does the venue have good relations with the press?

Is the venue represented at art expos or other such events?

Does the venue have a reputation for building careers?

Does the venue have contacts with museums or other institutions?

What is the venue's policy on financial split with an artist? 50/50?

What is the split on works sold through other spaces the venue has booked?

What is the venue's payment policy? 30 days? 60 days?

Is the venue's space appropriate for your art?

Is the venue computerized?

Is the venue online with the Internet?

Museums and Other Institutions

What is the focus of the museum?

What types of art are exhibited in the museum? Contemporary, traditional, regional, national, other?

What type of art does the museum collect?

Is the museum actively collecting now?

Does the museum have a collectors' council?

Does the museum have an exhibition committee?

What are the museum's presentation policies?

What are the museum's policies for accepting donations of art?

How long has the museum been in existence?

Does the museum hold fund-raising auctions?

How often does the museum change exhibitions?

How long does it take to book an exhibition?

Does the museum have a sales and rental gallery? What are the policies?

Does the museum have a gift shop that will consign artworks?

Does the museum present pre-organized exhibits?

Is the museum computerized?

Is the museum online with the Internet?

Is the museum appropriate for your work?

EXAMPLE: TELEPHONE RESEARCH WORKSHEET: GALLERIES, MUSEUMS, AND OTHER VENUES

Date of Contact *03/24/97*

Source of Listing *Personal*

Referred by *C. Kingston*

Name of Museum *Davis Modern Museum*

Affiliation ____________________

Goal of this call

Piece in Group Show _____ **Solo Show** _____

Representation _____ **Acquire for Collection** _____

Address *621 Doyle Carlton Dr.*

City, State, ZIP *Tampa, FL 33602*

Country *USA*

Telephone *(813) 555-6680*

Facsimile *(813) 555-4680*

E-mail *dlee@davismus.com*

Director *Duncan Lee*

Curator *Kennedy Benton*

Spoke with *Andrew Marquette*

Title *Assistant Director*

Hours *Tues. Sat. 10:00 am 5:00 pm*

What types of art are exhibited? *Paintings, sculpture, mixed media pieces*

What is the museum's focus? *Modern and contemporary and European art*

Do they show contemporary or traditional artists?

Contemporary _____ Traditional _____

What type of artists do they show?

Local _____ Regional _____

National _____ International _____

What artists are in their collection? *John Alan Lee, Mat Richards, Melanie Bellamore*

Is my work appropriate for this space? Yes _____ No _____

What are their presentation policies? *Submit color and b/w prints, labeled slides, (slide sheet only), print reviews, tear sheets. Current résumé a must.*

Other? ____

____

____

Presenting Your Work

At this point in your career planning, you will begin to come in contact with new people within the art community. Take a moment to tune up your communication skills. These guidelines are applicable whenever you contact another person for the purpose of achieving your career goals. Remember, first impressions occur within the first few seconds of meeting someone.

Preparing for Presentation

When making a presentation, keep a few rules in mind.

1. Do not show your work to a prospective venue unless your materials are in perfect order. Make sure all the materials are present, in the proper sequence, and in excellent condition.

QUICK TIP

Be confident about yourself and your work and others will be too.

2. Always respond in a timely manner. If you have solicited a prospective venue, it is your responsibility to provide everything you offered to the venue as promised and on time.
3. Be receptive to all possible options. You may present your work with one goal in mind, but the venue may perceive your work differently on the basis of its needs. Be open to what the venue offers, even if it varies from your original idea.
4. Be prepared to leave printed materials. As you have learned, always have a complete presentation package available. It is best to leave something that will remind your prospects of you and your work.
5. Keep the ball rolling. Once you make the first contact, keep pursuing. Never let a likely prospect cool off. A good salesperson knows that once a promising lead slips away one seldom gets a second chance.

Presenting in Person

The preferred way to present your work is in person. Ask to speak with the decision maker you previously identified. Arrange for an appointment with that person to present your work. You may have to be persistent to get an appointment, but if you express your awareness of how your work relates to the venue's focus and goals, barriers may come down.

On Someone Else's "Turf"

When you present your work on someone else's "turf," certain ground rules apply. Remember, galleries, museums, and universities are businesses, and the people who run them work on a tight schedule. Be considerate of their time. Keep your presentation brief and concise. A well-rehearsed presentation should last no longer than fifteen minutes. Include your presentation package and possibly one or two easily carried pieces.

How do you give the presentation? Be businesslike. Introduce yourself and shake hands. Thank the person at the outset for the opportunity to show your work.

To avoid misunderstandings, clarify your intentions at the beginning. For the gallery or dealer, you may be searching for representation. For a museum or other academic institution, state your desire to be included in an upcoming group or solo show or a collection or other exhibit. Your objectives will be dictated by the venue you are approaching. One objective, of course, is to solicit a professional's detached opinion of your art.

After the introduction, work briefly through your presentation materials. If you have a catalog, presentation binder, or brochure, offer it for the person's reference. The first impression of your work will come from your materials. Identify pieces available for exhibition, sale, loan, or other use.

Next, present the three color prints. The prints show how the artwork appears in a true setting. Let the person study the pictures. Follow up with the two black-and-white prints. The person will most likely be impressed with your readiness for press by having produced high quality black-and-white prints. The final step is to present your selected color slides.

Give the person time to absorb each piece of information and get the full impact of your work. Discuss positive points about your work as you present. If your work sells well, be sure to mention that fact. Your sales potential is important to the gallery's decision maker. Mention exhibitions where your work was well received. Do not hesitate to ask questions or solicit recommendations as to where your work may be best received.

If all goes well, close the meeting with a specific request: "I would like you to represent my work." Allow the person time to reflect. Do not say anything until he or she has had a chance to respond. Be open to what is said and, by all means, do not back the person into a corner by attacking with your question. If you receive a favorable response, you are on your way. If you receive a negative response, ask for any suggestions about how you might work together on a trial basis. Be prepared with a variety of well-thought-out alternatives. Think of ways to take advantage of this opportunity.

One artist I work with was very successful in a recent presentation by showing a dealer how he, the artist, would bring along new collectors to the gallery. These were people who had purchased his works in the past and were interested in new works and other artists. If you have a mailing list to offer, you can expand the dealer's base in exchange for expanding yours. If you know that one of the gallery's collectors has already purchased your work, be sure to mention that fact.

Remember, even the best preparation and presentation may result in a negative response. People may like your work, but not have anything to offer due to prior commitments. Or your work may not fit the gallery's focus. Do not be discouraged. Always ask for a referral. If the gallery shows any interest, put it on your mailing list, sending press information, invitations, and the like. Your mailings will keep you visible. Never be guilty of "out of sight—out of mind" behavior.

Graciously end the meeting with a next step statement, such as, "I will call you on Thursday," if that is what the person has suggested or, in respect to a referral, "I will call Mr. Hansen this afternoon." Always send a brief thank-you note for the person's time. The note shows appreciation as well as professionalism. Your thoughtfulness may go a long way when another opportunity arises for which your work may be suitable.

On Your Own "Turf"

Presenting in person and on your own "turf" is ideal if you have a studio that can comfortably display your work. This type of personal presentation also has guidelines.

When you schedule an appointment at your studio, plan to spend at least half an hour with your guest. Give the same presentation you would in his or her venue, except present a number of your actual works instead of photographs. Plan to display the art shown in your presentation materials. Put pieces not related to your presentation out of sight.

A prime example of losing an opportunity by presenting too much is an artist I know who had presented his work in New York and was particularly discouraged by the response from one of the city's more prestigious galleries. After the artist's presentation, the director, a famous and respected figure in the art community, recommended that the artist go home and take up a new profession. After looking at the work the artist had chosen to present, I could see the director's point. Confronted with thirty years' worth of the artist's best pieces, the director had every reason to be confused.

At the artist's request, I went to his studio to see his current work, which was mature, developed, and quite strong. Had he shown that work and only that work in New York, I felt certain that he would have received at least a mildly positive response, even if it didn't include an offer for an exhibition. Once again, we were back to the common question of where and how he might find a market for his art. I contacted an associate at a gallery in Los Angeles and had the artist send properly labeled slides, photographs, and support materials that focused exclusively on his more recent pieces. The gallery director was impressed, and agreed to book a show, but only after reviewing the work.

Although this artist had a large selection of his early work hung throughout his house, he had a separate studio where most of his current work was displayed. Having already discussed the reason for the New York gallery's negative response, I emphasized how vital it was that the artist show only the work that the director had viewed in the presentation package. The director's visit was not the time to distract his attention with a grand tour of the artist's life's work.

The day after the director visited the studio, the director called to say that he was withdrawing the show offer. The artist had chosen to give the the director the full tour, leaving him more confused than impressed. That tour was the end of a great opportunity for the artist.

Presenting through the Mail

Presenting your work through the mail is acceptable for venues beyond reasonable traveling distance from your studio. You do, however, lose some of the impact of presenting in person. Use your presentation materials to begin the relationship. Build the relationship through frequent calls to discuss scheduling an exhibition or obtaining representation. If your contact person feels comfortable with you, he or she will be more apt to assist or refer you to others in the area. If possible, try to make a trip to meet the venue's representative in person.

QUICK TIP

You only have one opportunity to make a good first impression.

Make it a rule to verify the legitimacy and interest of any venue before mailing presentation materials. Never send unsolicited materials to a venue. These packages are expensive. Unsolicited materials may not reach the person for whom they were intended. The materials might not even be returned to you—an expensive waste.

In your research, ask about the venue's policy on receiving an artist's presentation package. Obtain the name of the person who reviews such materials, and address the package accordingly. The qualification process, as discussed in the previous chapter, will enhance your chances of having your work reviewed. If you have a personal contact at the venue who knows the reviewer, ask permission to use his or her name when you approach the venue.

Keep a Log of Your Presentations

Presentation packages are somewhat costly to create. It is important to keep a current record of each venue and person who has your materials. Use your telephone research worksheet for this purpose.

Follow Up after Presentation

Follow up with your contact within four days after he or she should have received the materials. Ask whether the contact has reviewed your work and if you may set an appointment. Whether the response is positive or negative, always send a note thanking the contact for taking time to review your art.

EXAMPLE: PRESENTATION TRACKING WORKSHEET

Once you have organized and completed your presentation packages, you are ready to begin qualifying and presenting your work to targeted venues. Use this worksheet to track the sequence of steps within each presentation.

Contact Venue: *Sonova Gallery*

Action	**Date Completed**
Telephone research call. Initial introduction of artist to the qualified venue.	________
Personally present or mail the complete presentation package, including a personalized cover letter reflecting the key points discussed in the initial conversation.	________
Within at least four days of the presentation, call the package recipient to make sure the package was received (if mailed) and to determine if the recipient has had an opportunity to review your materials.	________
Send the appropriate follow-up letter as described in the chapter "Written Communications."	________
Continue to follow-up with the venue, calling and sending correspondence until receiving a final answer, either positive or negative. Remember, however, not to be overly pushy. Simply stay in regular contact with the venue.	________
If the venue makes a commitment, send a letter confirming all the terms of the agreement for exhibition, representation, or other activity. You may decide to allow the venue to keep your presentation package for sales and promotional purposes or you may allow the venue to keep the catalog and return the other materials for future presentations.	________
Send a thank-you note for the venue's time and efforts in reviewing your work. You may request your materials be returned, offering to let the venue keep your catalog for future reference.	________
If a certain amount of interest was expressed in your work but no commitment was made at this time, place this venue on your mailing list. Send regular notes, articles, invitations, and the like to your contact to keep the venue abreast of the progress your career is making. Above all else, actively work your mailing list.	________

***EXAMPLE:* PRESENTATION LOG WORKSHEET**

Returned ____ **Checked out** ____
Date of Presentation *02/20/97*
To Whom *Catherine Kingston*

Telephone *(213) 555-8910*
Location *The Contemporary Museum* G / M / I / Other
Presentation In Person ____ By a Rep ____ By Mail ____
Other ____
Materials Used Standard Package ____
Other *Asked to keep catalog for the museum's library*
Date Return Requested *03/01/97*
Date Materials Returned *Kept. Show pending.*

Returned ____ **Checked out** ____
Date of Presentation *02/25/97*
To Whom *Arnold James*
Telephone *(310) 555-3164*
Location *1754 Santa Monica, CA 92751* G / M / I / Other
Presentation In Person ____ By a Rep ____ By Mail ____
Other ____
Materials Used Standard Package ____
Other ____
Date Return Requested *03/15/97*
Date Materials Returned ____

Returned ____ **Checked out** ____
Date of Presentation *1/4/97*
To Whom *Swartnik Gallery*
Telephone *(310) 555-7862*
Location *Venice, CA* G / M / I / Other
Presentation In Person ____ By a Rep ____ By Mail ____
Other ____
Materials Used Standard Package ____
Other ____
Date Return Requested *1/28/97*
Date Materials Returned ____

7 WORKING WITH THE VENUE— THE BUSINESS OF BEING AN ARTIST

QUICK TIP

Follow through on your commitments in a timely manner.

Art as a career is also a business. You must be aware of and participate in various business practices established for your protection and that of the venue or representative. These practices include reading and signing contractual agreements, the documentation of art from venue to venue, and tracking fulfillment of your obligations to the venue and the venue's obligations to you. In this chapter, numerous standard forms and documents are provided for your use. Become familiar with each form, what it means, when to use it, and how it will be of benefit to you.

Read before You Sign

When you are approached with a contractual agreement, know the details of your obligation and what compensation you will receive for your efforts. Have an attorney review all contracts before signing. Prepare copies of your own standard agreements, such as those provided in this book, and confirm with an attorney that the agreements are valid should you use these documents in the course of business. Keep in mind that attorneys bill for their time. Be organized with your presentation of documents and know what your attorney will charge for this service. Don't be surprised by a large attorney's bill simply because you didn't ask about fees.

What Is Expected of You

Once you have obtained a representative, an exhibition, or funding, understand your obligations. Make a time line of when obligations are due, planning adequate lead time. Be prepared to frame and ship your works and insure them against damage. These are examples of details that will erode your profit margin if not addressed when you make your agreement. Each venue has different business practices, and it is your responsibility to learn about those practices when you qualify a venue. If you have done your homework, you should not have any unpleasant surprises.

What You Should Expect from Your Venue

When you obtain representation from a gallery, the cost of shipping the works to the gallery is most often your responsibility. The return shipment, however, is usually paid for by the gallery. Clarify these arrangements ahead of time. Insuring the works should be negotiated between you and the gallery at the onset.

Galleries generally pay for the promotion of the exhibition, including invitations, mailings, opening-night parties, press releases, and the like. You may find yourself pitching in when the gallery needs help. Be sure to have all expense reimbursements agreed to and signed before you begin. It is customary for all parties to be reimbursed for their promotion expenses before profits are distributed.

Some galleries will pay all or part of the costs of producing catalogs, brochures, and biography sheets. If they do, it is to your benefit. Remember, however, that the galleries may deduct these costs from the revenue before sharing the profits with you. Make sure you understand and agree to the arrangements ahead of time.

Payment for artworks sold is usually made within thirty days of the sale unless other arrangements have been agreed to. It is not unbusinesslike to request your share a few days after a buyer's check clears the gallery's bank. This arrangement should be covered in your contractual agreement.

Museums generally cover the expenses of shipping and insuring artwork both to and from the exhibition. Museums are not in the business of selling art but of exhibiting art. Museums will provide the necessary loan agreements, insurance documents, condition reports, and other supportive documents required for their purposes. Other academic venues vary in their policies regarding expenses they will pay, so ask before entering into an agreement with those venues.

Standard Documentation and Legal Forms

As an artist, you will sign contracts and agreements pertaining to your work. You must know the elements of a good contract. Even so, have an attorney review all agreements before you submit or sign them. Know what the contract obligates you to.

All contracts should include the specific names of all parties who are making the agreement, the signed consent of each party, the monetary or material consideration that will be made as a result of the agreement, and a detailed description of the obligation or actions being agreed to. This chapter discusses the following standard contracts:

Bill of Sale

Certificate of Authenticity

Provenance

Exhibition Agreement/Loan Agreement

Artist/Gallery Consignment Agreement

Condition Report

Insurance Agreement

Artwork Documentation for the Artist

CONTRACT SUMMARY

Bill of Sale

Who Provided to the purchaser of any work at the time of sale.

What Serves as a receipt and record for the transfer of funds for the ownership of an artwork. Notifies the purchaser of the artist's retainment of the rights for reproduction.

When Any time a purchase of work occurs.

Certificate of Authenticity

Who Provided to the purchaser of any work at the time of sale. (Some states permit the artist to provide this certificate after the sale. Consult your state's regulations.)

What Proof from the artist to the purchaser of the authenticity of the piece as a work of art by the artist as represented during the sale of the art.

When Any time a purchase of work occurs.

Provenance

Who Provided to the purchaser of any work at the time of sale.

What Documents the history of the piece, the transition of ownership from person to person, and the exhibition places of the piece. A chronological documentation of the exposure and ownership of a work of art.

When Any time a purchase of work occurs.

Agent Representation Contract

Who Provided for and to the artist when representation is obtained.

What Documents and confirms all obligations of the representative to the artist and of the artist to the representative, formalizing their relationship and reimbursement arrangements.

When When representation is agreed upon and prior to the beginning of any activity in accordance with this relationship.

Exhibition Agreement/Loan Agreement

Who Provided for and to the artist when artwork is to be transferred for the purpose of exhibition or sale.

What Documents the transfer of location of artwork without the transfer of ownership. Often provided to the artist by, for example, a museum. Should be used prior to the transfer of the art to any exhibition location.

When Prior to the shipment of artwork to an exhibition location.

Artist/Gallery Consignment Agreement

Who Provided for and to the artist when artwork is consigned for sale to a gallery.

What Documents the transfer of location of artwork for the purpose of sale without the transfer of ownership. Often provided to the artist by the gallery. Should be used prior to the transfer of the art to any exhibition location.

When At the time of delivery to the gallery.

Condition Report

Who Provided by the artist to the venue, usually a museum, at the time of shipment.

What Documents in detail the complete condition of the artwork at the time of shipment. It notes any damage, such as scratches and chips, or lack of damage and the cleanliness of the piece.

When Created at the time of delivery to the museum by the museum, and at the time of departure, noting the condition of the work at that time. Usually prepared by the museum registrar.

Insurance Agreement

Who Provided by the artist or the venue, whichever party has agreed to take responsibility for insuring the work in transit.

What Documents insurance of the artwork during transit.

When Prior to the crating and shipment of artwork.

EXAMPLE: BILL OF SALE

Place — *Richard Jones Gallery*
(Gallery, Museum, Art Show, Studio, or Business)

Sold to — *Dr. Arnold Smith*
(Name of Buyer)

20812 N. Fremont Avenue, San Francisco, CA
(Address of Buyer)

(415) 555-8451
(Phone Number of Buyer)

Sold by — *Robert Jones*
(Name of Seller—Artist or Authorized Dealer)

4763 E. Hampton, San Francisco CA
(Address of Seller)

(415) 555-8461
(Phone Number of Seller)

Description of Work — True Color
(Title)

Painting, oil on canvas 42" × 38"
(Subject, Media, Dimensions)

Blue painting by Hans Beckman
(Description)

Price — *$3,900.00*
(Complete Purchase Price)

Terms of Payment — *Paid in full upon delivery*

Reproduction Rights Reserved by the Artist

Dr. Arnold Smith
(Purchaser's Signature)

Richard Jones
(Artist or Authorized Dealer's Signature)

Date — *1/29/97*

EXAMPLE: CERTIFICATE OF AUTHENTICITY—ORIGINAL ARTWORK

Certificate of Authenticity

Artist *Hans Beckman*

Title True Color

Media *Oil on canvas*

Dimensions *36″ × 48″*

Year *1997*

Comments *Beckman considers this painting among his most important works of 1997.*

This is to certify that the artwork described above and attached hereto is an original work by the named artist.

Richard Jones *1/29/97*

(Artist or Authorized Dealer's Signature) (Date)

EXAMPLE: CERTIFICATE OF AUTHENTICITY—ORIGINAL PRINT

Certificate of Authenticity

Artist *Mark Brown*

Title Blue Sky

Media *Etching*

Dimensions *12" × 14"*

Publisher *Self*

Year *1997*

Number of authorized signed prints in this edition	*50*
Number of other editions	*0*
Number of artist proofs	*5*
Size of other editions	*N/A*
Number of unsigned proofs	*3*

Comments: *This etching was based on a group of works called the* Sky Series.

This is to certify that the artwork described above and attached hereto is an original print by the named artist.

Mark Brown *3/24/97*

(Artist or Authorized Dealer's Signature) (Date)

***EXAMPLE:* PROVENANCE**

This document serves as first issue of Provenance

Place Image Here

Type of Art	*Painting*
Artist	*Marty Esslinger*
Title	*Ladies*
Dimensions	*36" × 24"*
Year	*1997*

This artwork was completed by the artist in *June of 97* and was signed and so designated by the artist as to the year of completion and authenticity.

This artwork was acquired by *Thomas Smith* (Seller) in *1997* (Year of Purchase).

Ownership of the above described work was transferred to:

Sally Bird
(Name of Buyer)

3146 Cunningham, Berkeley, CA 93846
(Address of Buyer)

(415) 555-4126
(Phone Number of Buyer)

on *3/10/97* (Sale Date) for the sum of: *One thousand six hundred dollars ($1,600.00)* (Purchase Price).

As of this date, ownership of this painting remains with *Sally Bird*.

Thomas Smith
(Seller's Signature)

3/10/97
(Date)

EXAMPLE: EXHIBITION AGREEMENT

This Exhibition Agreement is made and entered into to be effective as of the *3rd* day of *June* 19*97*, by and between *Georgia Klum*, sometimes referred to as "Artist" and *Greg Gaynor* sometimes referred to as "Authorized Representative" providing exhibition space for the works described hereto, sometimes referred to as "Space."

The purpose of this agreement is to set forth the understandings governing the agreed to exhibition by Artist of the described works of art in the Exhibition Space.

Artist

Georgia Klum
(Name of Artist)

1934 Jane Street, San Diego, CA 92659
(Address)

(619) 555-9486
(Telephone)

Exhibition Space

Gaynor Gallery
(Name of Space)

4729 Beach Street, San Diego, CA 92642
(Location of Space)

Greg Gaynor
(Authorized Representative for Space)

Artworks for Exhibition

Title	Media	Dimensions	Year
Blue Tree	*Acrylic on canvas*	*19" × 22"*	*1997*
Grey Dog	*Watercolor on paper*	*33" × 46"*	*1997*

Duration *3/24/97* to *4/2/97*

(Starting Date of Exhibition) (Ending Date of Exhibition)

Monday to Friday, 9:00 A.M. to 6:00 P.M.; Saturday 10:00 A.M. to 5:00 P.M.
(Exhibition Hours Open to the Public)

No works shall be removed from the Space's premises until sold or returned to the Artist, unless otherwise agreed upon in writing.

Installation Artist / Space (circle one) shall be solely responsible for the installation of the exhibition. Installation shall begin on *3/18*, 19 *97* and be completed by *3/23*, 19 *97*. All final installation decisions shall be the sole responsibility of the Space staff. Materials required for installation, including mountings, tape, pins, nails, and similar items as required are the responsibility of the Artist / Space *(circle one)*.

Delivery Artworks are to arrive at the Space on *3/18*, 19 *97* by *8* am/pm. Artworks shall be confirmed as received by *Joseph*.

Shipment of the works to the Space shall be arranged by *Joseph* and paid for by *N/A* including insurance. Artist shall advise the Space in writing of the prices and insurance values for each work to be exhibited by *3/16*, 19 *97*.

Insurance Space shall insure the works for the values assigned by the Artist from the period when the works arrive at the Space until the works are removed from the Space. The Space is responsible for security of all works while present on the Space premises. The Space represents that it is in sound repair and shall be responsible for damage to the works as a result of structural defects, water damage, vandalism, theft, or the like. The Space shall exercise reasonable care in dealing with the works.

The Space shall maintain all public and exhibition areas in a good state of repair, clean and orderly.

Promotions The following publicity and promotions shall be provided for this exhibition:

x	Invitations	Artist / Space / Shared
x	Press Releases	Artist / Space / Shared
x	Public Service Announcements	Artist / Space / Shared
____	Advertisements	Artist / Space / Shared
____	Posters	Artist / Space / Shared
x	Brochure/Catalog	Artist / Space / Shared
____	Artist's Reception	Artist / Space / Shared
____	Other ____________________	Artist / Space / Shared

The costs of promotions shall be reimbursed to the Artist and/or Space as agreed upon hereto:

Within seven days of the close of the exhibition the gallery will pay all monies owed to artist.

Deinstallation Artist / Space (circle one) shall be solely responsible for the deinstallation of the exhibition. Deinstallation shall begin on _4/25_, 19 _97_ and be completed by _4/25_, 19 _97_.

Artworks not sold during the exhibition are to be returned to the artist by _4/26_, 19 _97_ by _8_ am/pm. Return shipment of the works will be arranged by _Space_ and paid for by _Space_, including insurance based on the values provided at time of delivery.

Remuneration In remuneration for exhibiting and selling the Artist's works, the Space shall receive a _50_ percent commission on the Net / Gross (circle one) sale of the art.

For commissions based on net sales values, the following expenses shall be subtracted from the sale revenues prior to determining the total commission to be paid the Space:

Cost of framing

Artist is to receive the monies from the sale of the work within _7_ days of receipt from the purchaser. Delinquency in payment will activate a _0_ percent penalty to be subtracted from the Space's commission.

Amendments Amendments, modifications, supplements or changes to this Agreement shall be in writing and signed by both parties.

Termination of Agreement by Both Parties Either party may terminate this Agreement by giving to the other party sixty (60) days notice in writing.

Laws Governing Agreement This agreement shall be governed by and construed in accordance with the laws of the State of California.

Both parties agree that this represents the entire understanding between them, and that it shall be a binding contract upon the signature of the Artist and an authorized representative of the Space.

Georgia Klum	*5/24/96*
(Artist or Authorized Dealer's Signature)	(Date)
Greg Gaynor	*5/24/96*
(Authorized Space Representative)	(Date)

Page 3 of 3

EXAMPLE: CONSIGNMENT AGREEMENT

It is hereby agreed between ___*Justine M. Resnik*___, hereinafter referred to as "owner" of the artworks described in Schedule A, attached hereto, and ___*Patrick Decrona*___, hereinafter referred to as "dealer," that dealer shall exhibit and offer the described artwork for sale to dealer's clients under the following conditions:

1. The works hereby consigned to the dealer as agent for the owner and described herein are priced at net to owner on the attached list. All works shall remain the property of the owner unless and until they are purchased by collectors or the dealer.
2. The works shall be exhibited or made available for inspection by prospective purchasers by the dealer from _*June 23*_, 19_*97*_ until this agreement is terminated by owner or dealer upon thirty (30) days' written notice to the other party.
3. The owner will assist the dealer by framing all works hereby consigned. The owner's incurred costs in framing will be returned to the owner in addition to the sale price of the work of art.
4. The dealer will pay the owner the net price hereby established and agreed upon per the attached inventory sheet on any works sold by the dealer. Notice of all sales will be given to the owner at the conclusion of each month and payment of all monies due shall be made not more than thirty days after the receipt of payment by the dealer. The dealer assumes full risk of nonpayment by the purchaser.
5. During the term of this agreement and during shipping from and to the owner, the dealer shall cause all of owner's work consigned to the dealer to be insured to the benefit of owner against any and all loss in an amount equal to the owner's net amount.
6. No unsold works shall be removed from the dealer's premises until the works are sold to a purchaser unless agreed upon in writing.
7. The owner shall have the right to inventory all consigned works at reasonable times and to obtain a full accounting for any works not present at the dealer's premises at such time.
8. The owner, as copyright owner of the hereby consigned works, reserves all rights to the reproduction of the works in any manner. This restriction shall be indicated by the dealer in writing on all sales invoices and memoranda. However, the owner will not withhold permission for the reproduction of such works for promotional purposes if all such reproductions are submitted to owner for approval prior to any printing and distribution of said promotional materials.

Page 1 of 3

9. This agreement shall at all times be governed by the laws of the state of *New York* .

Justine M. Resnik *3/9/97*
(Artist's Signature) (Date)

JUSTINE M. RESNIK
(Artist's Printed Name)

4172 Broadway
(Artist's Street Address)

New York, NY 38614, USA
(Artist's City, State, ZIP, and Country Address)

(212) 555-9482
(Artist's Telephone Number(s))

Thomas Wonder *3/9/97*
(Authorized Representative's Signature) (Date)

THOMAS WONDER
(Authorized Representative's Printed Name)

T - Wonder Gallery
(Venue Name)

35 Solo Street
(Venue Street Address)

New York, NY 75421, USA
(Venue City, State, ZIP, and Country Address)

(212) 555-9631
(Venue Telephone Number(s))

Page 2 of 3

SCHEDULE A

Total Number of Pieces Consigned under This Agreement: 3

x Under Stress — *1997*
(Title) (Year Created)

Painting, oil on canvas, 19″ × 19″
(Subject, Media, Dimensions)

Landscape with figure
(Description)

x Water Can — *1997*
(Title) (Year Created)

Painting on board, acrylic on paper, 12″ × 16″
(Subject, Media, Dimensions)

Landscape with metal can
(Description)

x Burnt Car — *1997*
(Title) (Year Created)

Painting, acrylic on board, 40″ × 30″
(Subject, Media, Dimensions)

City scene with burnt auto
(Description)

____

(Title) (Year Created)

(Subject, Media, Dimensions)

(Description)

Page 3 of 3

EXAMPLE: **CONDITION REPORT**

Name of Lender	*Thomas Hornsby*
Name of Institution	*Fry University*
Address	*1941 Elm Street*
City, State, ZIP	*Seattle, WA 94371*

Artist	*Brad Hornsby*
Title	Blue Flag
Dimensions	*96" × 58"*
Media	*Oil on canvas*
Year	*1962*

This report is to document the condition of the above described artwork at this time of receipt *Nov. 6* , 19*96* by the institution.

Condition of frame	*Good*
Condition of paint, canvas, etc. indicating any minor blemishes	*There is a small scratch on the upper left corner of the painting.*
Report any abnormal condition of the artwork	*Other than the scratch, everything else is in good condition.*

Indicate by photo or diagram any and all suspicious or damaged areas. Attach said documentation to this report and lender's copy. Immediately notify lender of damage.

Roberts Blevins	*Fry University*
(Registrar's Signature)	(Institution)

EXAMPLE: ARTWORK DOCUMENTATION FOR THE ARTIST

Type of Work	*Painting*
Category	*Paintings*
Catalog Number	*124*
Artist	*Brad Hornsby*
Title	Blue Flag
Description	*Large painting of a flag*
Size	*96" × 60"*
Medium	*Oil*
Completion Date	*1962*
Date Acquired by	*Thomas Hornsby; 1962*
Framed	Yes ____ No ____

Exhibits

(Location)	**(Dates of Exhibition)**		
Blum Museum, Dallas, TX	*June 1975*	to	*July 1975*
		to	
		to	

Scholarship	Yes ____ No ____
Condition Report on File	Yes ____ No ____

Estimated Value	*$14,000.00*
Appraisal Value	*$14,000.00*
Date Sold	*N /A*
Name of Buyer	*N /A*
Address	*N /A*
City, State, ZIP	*N /A*
Sales Price	*N /A*

Place Your Image Here

8 PROMOTIONS

In promoting your artwork, you have several interrelated goals. First, you want to arouse the interest of the art community. Second, you want members of that community to become sufficiently interested that they will come to see and experience your work. Finally, you want those who do see your work to talk to others about it. To create this excitement about your work, you will employ a variety of means ranging from printed materials, printed and electronic press, and special events to personal networking. Many of your options are not expensive but simply require ingenuity and perseverance on your part.

QUICK TIP

Staying on top of promotions will make a difference in your success.

Artists often are intimidated by the idea of promoting their work. The process you have undertaken to qualify and present your work to venues has been a form of promotion. You have been spreading the word to a focused audience. Promotion on a larger scale simply broadens this audience. Once you have achieved a goal, it is time to tell the world that something very exciting is happening. You must interest the art community in seeing and experiencing your work. You cannot isolate yourself and your art and expect your work to be recognized by the art community. Do not rely solely on others to make you visible and promote you. You must stay on top of what is happening.

Who Is Responsible for Promotions?

You are! It is your art and the success of your career that are at issue. You must actively participate in this process. You will find that many venues are willing and able to take responsibility for promoting their events, but you must be ready to pitch in creatively, actively, and in some cases, financially. You want to take advantage of any and all exposure. Do not expect everyone to provide the same quality of promotion of your works that you would.

There are different levels of promotion. One level focuses on a short-term goal—an upcoming exhibition, for example. Another level of promotion deals with your personal long-term goals, for example, raising the importance of your art to such a level as to make it worthy of academic exhibitions, such as in museums. Each type of goal calls for different activities.

Before You Begin—Keys to Promotional Success

Before you actually begin any promotional program, keep a few rules in mind.

Organization

Starting out and staying organized will be the key to success. Plan each promotional activity carefully, taking into consideration the timing and cost of each step in your plan. Use the checklist provided on page 140 to organize what needs to be done.

Know Your Audience

Depending on the audience you have selected, certain types of promotional activities will be more cost effective and give you better results than others. Know your audience. Avoid using a shotgun approach to distributing your materials. It is important to know where your materials are being presented and who your audience is.

Mailing Lists

Keep a current mailing list of all people who have expressed interest in or collected your work. Include in your list local art writers and critics, targeted venue staff members, members of the press, influential art patrons, and prominent members of the art community. Continuously update your mailing lists with new names and new information.

QUICK TIP

Keep updating your mailing list.

Resources for obtaining mailing lists can be found in a variety of places. For example, review the names listed in your guest book from an exhibition. Specialized mailing lists can be purchased from publications and organizations. Local non-profit organizations are a good source of specialized lists. Many artists have found that the people on their mailing lists are their best buyers.

Mailing lists are most easily kept on a computer so that you can update them easily and print labels by categories quickly. Many reasonably priced software packages designed for just such purposes are available. Even if you don't have access to a computer, you must keep your lists up-to-date.

Follow Up

Following up on your activities is imperative. Personal contact with your audience will always enhance the effectiveness of your promotion. For example, when you send a press release to a local writer or critic, it is best to also call to confirm receipt of the materials and to answer any questions. You may wish to take advantage of the opportunity to personally invite the writer to the opening reception.

Perseverance

At first you may feel as if your efforts are not being rewarded. In time, however, the barriers will fall. Observe the responses you are getting from your materials, adjust what needs to be adjusted, and simply keep at it. Keep an open mind and learn from each activity. You will eventually become part of the mainstream art community.

Promotions for Scheduled Events

Invitations, press releases, public service announcements, editorials, posters, tear sheets, catalogs, and brochures are all promotional materials that can be used to elicit interest in scheduled events. Each item is used for a different purpose and is directed to a different audience. Plan to use one or more of these techniques to advertise your event.

Invitations

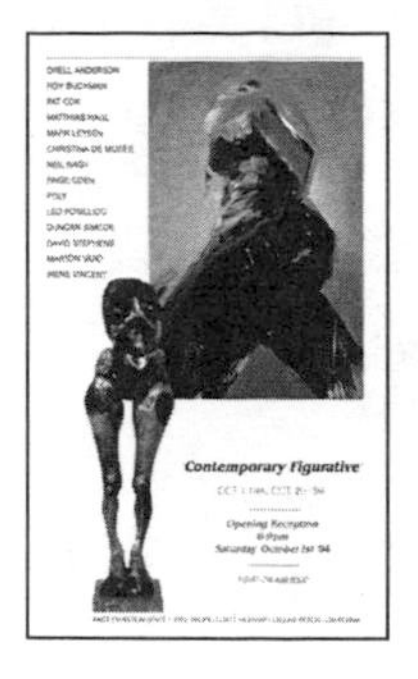

Invitations are sent to entice people to come to your show. You should send invitations to members of the art community, including university faculty, museum curators and directors, gallery dealers, art organizations, collectors, and general patrons. These people will help to spread the word about the event for you.

An invitation can take on almost any form and can range greatly in price. If you have a large budget, you can print a card with a full-color image of a piece from your show on one side and invitational information on the other. Avoid being gimmicky. The invitation, as should all your other materials, should reflect upon you as a professional and not be too glitzy.

Cost-effective Invitation Format

It is my opinion, however, that there are many alternatives to a full-color, professionally printed invitation. These less expensive invitations will allow you to apply your funds to something more permanent, such as your catalog or brochure. An invitation will be used for a single event while your catalog or brochure will be used again and again to build your career.

A cost-effective and impressive invitation can be made from an 8-1/2" × 11" sheet of paper properly formatted, printed, and folded. A sample of such an invitation is shown on page 135. The idea behind this invitation design is to fold the page so that it ends up looking like a fold-over card. Use a small white or colored sticker to seal the invitation. You can use a few special touches to give greater sophistication to this basic invitation design, but remember not to make the invitation look too commercial unless, of course, that is the marketplace you are targeting.

You may consider using a full-color versus a black-and-white image on your invitation. Color is preferred, but don't be upset if your budget only allows for black and white. Your venue may have an invitation budget for the exhibition. You may wish to contribute to this budget to upgrade the quality of the invitation, for example, from a black-and-white image to a color image. Above all, be creative.

When to Mail the Invitation

Invitations are generally mailed out two weeks prior to the opening dates of the exhibition. If mailed too soon, the invitations may get lost; too late, people may have conflicting plans. In planning when to mail your invitations, consider how long the postal service will take to deliver the piece. Mail moves more quickly in some areas than in others.

EXAMPLE: INVITATION WORKSHEET

The image should appear on the front of the invitation; the text should appear on the back.

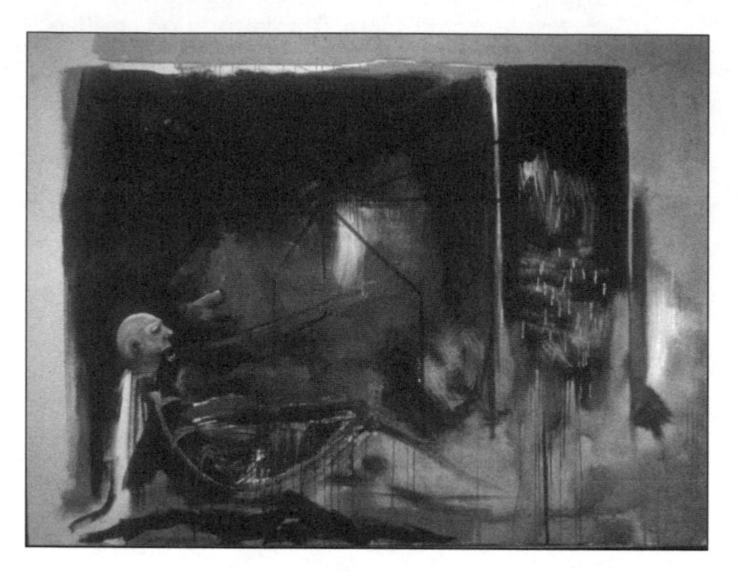

Your Name	*Jerome Gastaldi*
Event Name	Television Autocracy
Event Dates	*October 18 - November 28, 1997*
Artist's Reception (Day, Date, Time)	*Sunday, October 18, 2:00–5:00 P.M.*
Location Name	*Brumschmelt Gallery*
Location Address	*5930 Michaelson Drive, Los Angeles, CA 90013*
Contact Phone	*(213) 555-7891*
Daily Hours	*Tuesday–Saturday 11:00 A.M. to 5:00 P.M.*
Image Title	Tel Aviv (72" × 96")

Press Releases

The press release is used to inform newspapers, art writers, art critics, art magazines, and other publications about your exhibition. It is most effective to direct the press release to two or three individuals within each targeted publication. These people rely on press releases to keep them up-to-date on news. Your gallery may be experienced in dealing with the press, but make sure what the gallery sends out is accurate and projects the right image. The press release should be directed from the exhibiting venue to the press and not from the artist. I think it is important to know at all times what is being stated about you and your work.

QUICK TIP

Don't be afraid to call. The squeaky wheel gets the grease!

Create a list of all newspapers and magazines distributed in the geographical areas you want to target. Local press associations often publish inexpensive booklets with this information completely outlined. You can usually find these booklets in your local library. Review your list and remove any publications that do not cover the art community. Your list should now be down to a manageable size and contain from ten to thirty publications, depending on the population of your targeted community.

For each publication, identify the two or three people who cover the art scene. These people may include an art critic, an art editor, a community events editor, a managing editor, or the chief editor. Call each publication to determine who handles press releases for upcoming art events. Ask for the proper spelling of his or her name, exact title, and the address to mail the release to. Once you have this information, add them to your "press" mailing list.

Format of a Press Release

A press release is written in a succinct fashion with all the key information very clearly stated. The release should be printed on a sheet of paper that has "Press Release" or "News Release" prominently spelled out across the top. Include the following information:

Name of Venue

Venue Phone Number

Artist Name(s)

Event Name

Event Dates

Name of Venue Representative

Title of the Venue Representative

Artist's Reception Day, Date, and Time

Brief Statement about the Event

Brief Statement about the Artist(s)

Venue Address

Venue Operating Hours

Avoid using flowery language in your press release. Keep your approach simple. The media appreciate concise, clear writing. For best results, laser print the release as you would any other presentation piece, and make the additional copies on a quality photocopier.

Mail the press release in an 8-1/2" × 11" envelope, addressed with typed or printed labels. Do not fold the press release. Use the return address of the venue and not your address.

When to Mail the Press Release

Each publication has its own deadlines. Magazines often stop accepting releases two to three months prior to publication. Newspapers are far more flexible with their deadline dates, generally two weeks prior to the issue date. As you call each publication to identify the proper contacts, ask about deadlines for submitting a press release. Note the dates on your list. You may even choose to organize your press list in order of deadline dates.

Send a Photograph

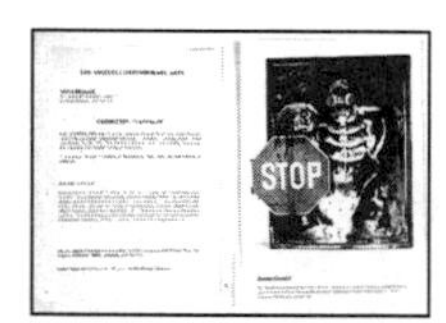

For the art writers and critics and for those general-interest magazines that often print pictures of artworks, include one or two of your best 8" × 10" or 8-1/2" × 11" black-and-white photographs. When publications need to fill space with a photograph, they may well use yours because it is readily available and free. Do not, however, go to the great expense of enclosing a photograph with every press release. Send photographs only to those publications that print pictures of artworks.

Always properly label the picture in case it becomes separated from your package. I also recommend using a sheet of paper laser printed with your name, title of the painting, a brief statement about the exhibition, exhibition dates, location, and contact phone number taped to the photograph just as it would appear in a picture caption. This information makes it very easy for publications to use the print. A sample of a photograph prepared this way is shown on the following pages.

***EXAMPLE:* PRESS RELEASE**

LOS ANGELES CONTEMPORARY ARTS

PRESS RELEASE

For additional information, contact:
Jie Shim, Director, (213) 555-1525

EXHIBITION *GASTALDI*

LOS ANGELES, CA—A one-man exhibition of fine art by the artist Jerome Gastaldi opens at the Los Angeles Contemporary Arts Gallery, Los Angeles, California, on June 15 and runs through July 3, 1997. This exhibition will feature recent works, including his paintings with integrated video monitors playing his productions.

A reception for the artist is scheduled for the evening of Friday, June 19, from 6:00 P.M. to 9:00 P.M.

JEROME GASTALDI

Gastaldi was born in Oakland, California, in 1945. He is a painter and a mixed media artist. Gastaldi's 10' × 8' integrated video painting, *Electronic Blessing whether You Like It or Not,* includes nine television monitors in the shape of a cross all playing a video of a Catholic priest giving a blessing. The piece was selected for the international exhibition, Images Du Futur 1997, in Montreal, Canada, which opened Ma, 1997. He will also be showing at the Southern California Art Institute in Orange County from June 11 through July 10 and at the South Bay Contemporary Museum in Torrance, California, from June 27 through August 6.

The Los Angeles Contemporary Arts Gallery (LACA) is located at 3630 Wilshire Blvd., Los Angeles, CA 90010. Telephone: (213) 555-1525.

Gallery hours are 11:00 A.M. to 7:00 P.M., Monday through Saturday.

EXAMPLE: GASTALDI, "ONE NATION OVER GOD"

JEROME GASTALDI "One Nation Over God" is a featured work at the one man exhibition of paintings, sculpture and integrated video paintings opening June 15 at Los Angeles Contemporary Arts Gallery (LACA). The exhibition runs through July 3.

Los Angeles Contempory Arts

QUICK TIP

You may label the back of the photo or attach a separate sheet of paper to the photo with information as this example shows.

***EXAMPLE:* COST-EFFECTIVE INVITATION**

This folded format is a cost-effective way to print a one-sided invitation.

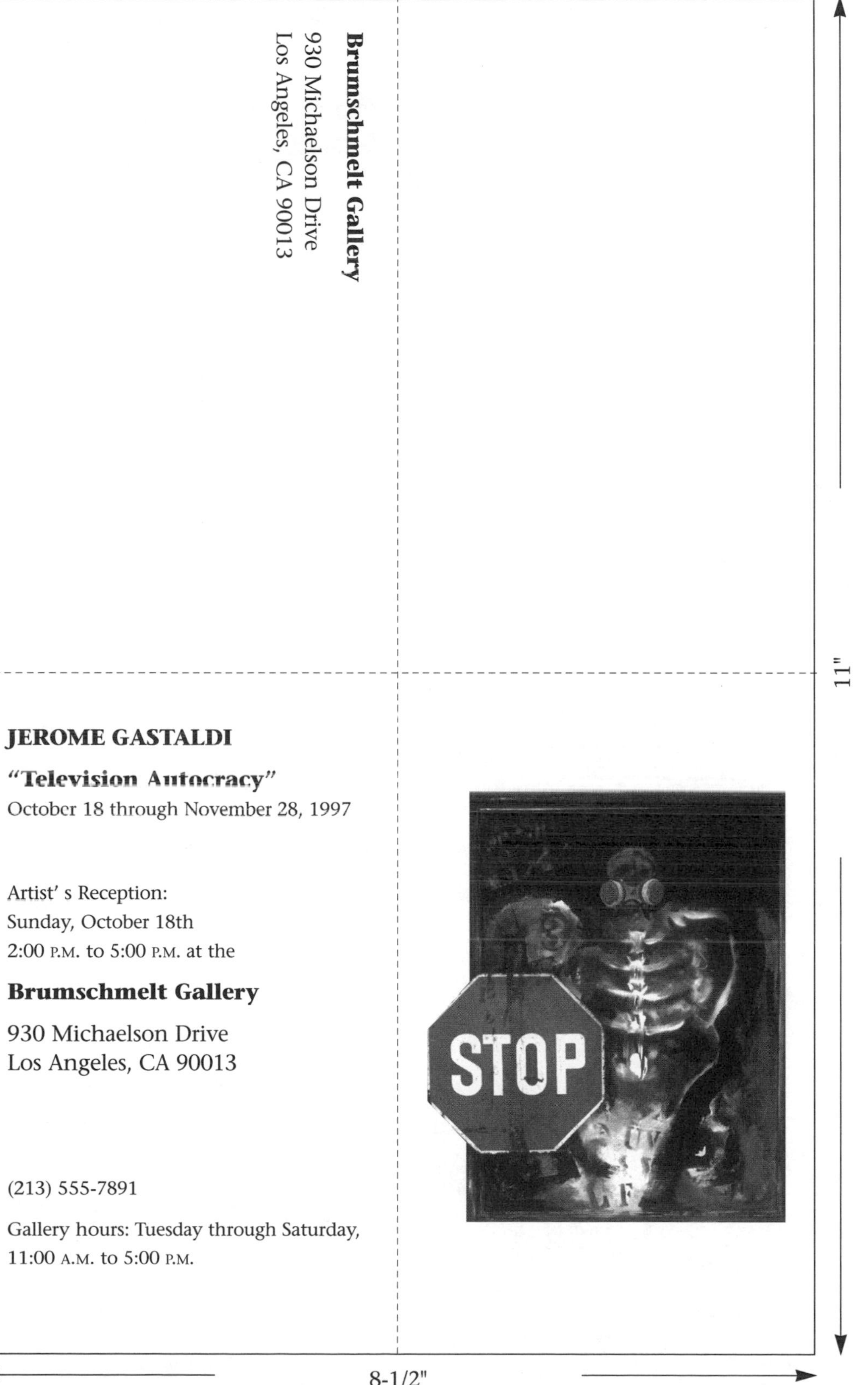

Brumschmelt Gallery
930 Michaelson Drive
Los Angeles, CA 90013

JEROME GASTALDI

"Television Autocracy"
October 18 through November 28, 1997

Artist' s Reception:
Sunday, October 18th
2:00 P.M. to 5:00 P.M. at the

Brumschmelt Gallery

930 Michaelson Drive
Los Angeles, CA 90013

(213) 555-7891

Gallery hours: Tuesday through Saturday,
11:00 A.M. to 5:00 P.M.

EXAMPLE: PRESS RELEASE WORKSHEET

Venue Name *Los Angeles Contemporary Arts*

PRESS RELEASE

For additional information, contact:

Contact Name *Jie Shim, Director*

Contact Phone Number *(213) 555-1525*

Artist's Last Name or Exhibition Name GASTALDI

City, State Location *Los Angeles, CA*

Brief Statement about Event

A one-man exhibition of fine art by the artist, Jerome Gastaldi, opens at the Los Angeles Contemporary Arts Gallery, Los Angeles, California on June 15 and runs through July 3, 1997. This exhibition will feature recent works, including his paintings with integrated video monitors playing his productions.

Event Dates *June 15 through July 3, 1997*

Reception Day, Date, Time *Friday, June 19, 6:00 P.M. to 9:00 P.M.*

Brief Artist Statement

Born in Oakland, CA, 1945. Painter and mixed media artist. Gastaldi's 10' × 8' integrated video painting, Electronic Blessing . . . , nine television monitors in the shape of a cross all playing a video of a Catholic priest giving a blessing. The piece selected Intl. exh., Images du Futur 1997, Montreal, Canada, opened May 1997. Also showing SCAI in OC from June 11 through July 10 and SBCM in Torrance, CA, from June 27 through Aug. 6.

Venue Name Repeated *The Los Angeles Contemporary Arts Gallery (LACA)*

Complete Venue Address *3630 Wilshire Blvd., Los Angeles, CA 90010 (213) 555-1525*

Venue Hours *Mon.–Sat., 11:00 A.M.–7:00 P.M.*

Format the text to emphasize the key pieces of information.

Public Service Announcements

Many artists do not realize the ease with which they can promote an event through radio and television. Many stations broadcast public service announcements regarding events occurring in their audience's area.

Create a list of all the radio and television stations that broadcast to the geographic area you are targeting. Don't overlook the local college and university stations. Again, local press associations often publish inexpensive booklets that you can find in your local public library with complete information about the stations.

For each station, identify the person who coordinates the public service announcements. Call the station to determine who handles the public service announcements. This person may be the station manager or the public services coordinator. Ask for the proper spelling of his or her name, exact title, and the address to mail the announcement to. Often, the station will tell you to facsimile the announcement. Once you have this information, add it to your media mailing list.

Format of a Public Service Announcement

The major stations have press kits for writing public service announcements. Request that a kit be sent to you at least one month before you are ready to approach the station. The rules for writing, presentation, and clarity for a press release also apply to public service announcements.

When to Facsimile the Public Service Announcement

Each station will have its own deadline date, generally, one to two weeks prior to the event. As you contact each station, ask what the deadlines are for submitting a public service announcement. Note the dates on your list.

Editorial—Free Press with a Punch

Receiving editorial review is not as difficult as one might think. It requires a good press release with a "hook" or something about your exhibition that is different. The release should pique the writer's curiosity and inspire him or her to learn more about you and your work. Personal contact and rapport with the critic or writer you wish to have review your work is also helpful. Do not be afraid to contact the writer; all he or she can say is no. Push your gallery to do the work of contacting the press as well.

This type of promotion takes planning. Begin by sending a press release to the writer. Follow it up with a personal phone call inviting him or her to attend your reception. Send a follow-up invitation as a reminder of your gesture. If the writer would like to see your exhibit, be available. Your gallery should be helpful in making the contact as well, but do not rely on it.

Be attentive. Introduce the writer to your dealer if they do not already know each other. If you have a catalog or brochure, give a signed copy to the writer. After the show, send the writer a thank-you note for attending.

Establishing rapport with a writer can open up new opportunities. Do not directly ask the writer to write about your show. Let your dealer be the one who urges the writer to do a story on you. Even if you are involved behind the scenes, you do not want the writer to get the impression you are trying to promote yourself.

Special Events

Everyone likes a party, and a smart artist will know how to use this appeal to his or her benefit. Several types of events can bring the art community to see your work. The most common event is an artist's reception held on the opening day of an exhibition. The reception can be simple, with a few refreshments, or more elaborate.

You can also use other types of events, as described below, to promote your work.

Charity Events

Charity events, including auctions, dinners, fund-raisers, and the like, are excellent opportunities for you to have your work seen. Donate your work to worthy causes. Patrons of such events tend to be in tune with the art world and will be interested in the art for their personal collections. Such functions can open up future possibilities for you.

Open House at Your Studio

An open house at your studio is an invitation to come see your art in your work environment. It can be arranged much like an artist's reception. The type of open house you hold may reflect the type of art you create. Be creative and you will find that your budget will go far.

An open house should not be held too frequently, probably only two times a year. Depending upon the area you live in—for example, a metropolitan area as opposed to a rural area—entertaining by an artist may be done more or less frequently. You may want to team up with a dealer during your open house because it is easier for the dealer to make sales while you mingle with guests.

Use your mailing list. Many collectors like to go to the artist's studio to meet the artist and see what new pieces are available and ones that are being created. Be sure to mail personal invitations to your guests well in advance of the event. Do not invite the media to your open house. Your open house is not a news event, and the media may view your invitation as an attempt to curry favor with them.

Be selective about what art pieces you show. Have only your strongest pieces, and possibly a few in the process of being created, out for your guests to view. Put away any pieces that are not part of your current body of work because such pieces may confuse your guests about your work. Recall the lesson learned by the artist who showed the dealer his entire collection of works and was subsequently rebuffed.

Demonstrations at Art Fairs/Public Places

Commercial artists can use demonstrations at art fairs and expositions to put themselves before the public. The idea is to be out in front of the public attending an art event. You never know who may be interested in purchasing your work or what dealers will offer you an opportunity to exhibit in their galleries.

Lectures

The fine artist can use a similar opportunity to get exposure by lecturing at colleges, universities, art organizations, and similar places. Feel free to write a brief press release about your upcoming lecture. The press often picks up on events such as lectures.

Long-term Promotional Options

Once again, there are different levels of promoting. One level deals with an immediate need. Your activities are focused on a short-term goal, for example, an upcoming exhibition. Another level of promotion deals with your personal long-term goals, for example, raising the importance of your art to such a level as to make it worthy of a museum exhibition. Different activities can be undertaken to achieve your long-term goals. I think it is important to keep your long-term goals in mind.

Newsletters

A newsletter is a relatively inexpensive way to keep your audience abreast of the progression of your career. It allows you to talk about new works, published works, upcoming events, awards and honors you have received, and any other information you feel your audience will be interested in knowing.

An artist's newsletter should be well written and nicely formatted. Many good books have been published on how to write and produce newsletters. Invest a few dollars in one of these books, study it, and keep it at your desk for reference.

Mail the newsletter to the people on your mailing list. Have copies of your most recent letter available as handout material at your exhibitions and at galleries that sell your works. You may also consider sending a copy of the newsletter to your press contacts. The newsletter is a promotional tool to keep your name and your work in front of the people.

When writing a newsletter, be careful not to make it sound like a vanity piece. The language should be informative and interesting, not boastful. Have someone whose opinion you respect read and critique your newsletter before you print and distribute it.

Newsletters do not necessarily have to be printed by a professional print shop. If you have access to a computer with a laser printer and a desktop publishing software package, you can prepare an impressive publication. Print a master copy on your laser printer and then take the master to a copy service to be photocopied. You can make the newsletter as elaborate or as simple as you wish. The key will be to have the recipient view the newsletter as a professional publication and find the information interesting and worthwhile to read.

Videos

In this age of electronic media, many artists have begun to produce videos about themselves and their works. These videos are short presentations designed to give the viewer an understanding of the artist and their works.

If you are interested in producing a video, I strongly advise you consult with a production company that is knowledgeable about artists' promotional videos. Using a homemade video for promotion can give the impression of amateurism.

When properly done, producing videos can be expensive. I advise holding off on this type of project until you have a budget for it. When you do have a video produced, do not take shortcuts because the result will not be professional. Consider using the resources of your local college or university to keep down costs.

Advertising

Advertising, as with videos, can be quite expensive. You have many other options to promote yourself without going to such expense. But, if you do feel the need to advertise your work in a magazine or newspaper, I suggest consulting a person familiar with targeting your market to help you design and place your advertisements.

You will want to plan carefully when and where to place your advertisements. An advertising person familiar with the art market and the art publications should be able to direct you to negotiating a good location for your ad in different magazines. The inside covers and outside back covers are more expensive than advertisements within the body of the publication.

I have discussed the benefits of advertising with many dealers. Most dealers feel that the only benefit they received from advertising was name recognition. If you do advertise, you must do so regularly. Running an ad in just one or two issues will have little, if any, impact. For the most part, however, I think you should spend your promotional dollars on other options unless your venue shares the cost. I do not recommend putting an advertisement in a magazine or newspaper with your own phone and address as it looks too self-promotional. Try to work with a gallery.

Submitting Articles to Publications

If your writing skills are good or you can team up with someone whose are, you may consider submitting articles to various magazines. These articles can discuss your work, issues confronted by your work, events and benefits supported by your work, or any topic that is appropriate to the focus of the magazine to which you are submitting the article. The process of having an article accepted by a magazine can be frustrating. But if you persevere, you will eventually have success.

Television and Radio Shows

Now we are talking about the artist who is really willing to put it all on the line. If you are, you should begin to identify news and talk shows that feature segments on the arts. In my area, for example, there is a public television show funded by a grant from a regional arts foundation. Its focus is to inform and enlighten the community about the arts. Shows of this type would be likely candidates for you to research. Large metropolitan areas abound with these types of shows. Television interviews are also an inexpensive way to have a video made about you and your work. Consider approaching your local cable stations and the television and radio stations at your local colleges and universities.

Begin by sending a public service announcement to the show's producer. Then, in a fashion similar to your standard venue presentation, you will begin to solicit the show. Learn about the show's focus, what it is trying to achieve. Watch the show to see what kind of people and events it covers. Develop your presentation to correspond to the show's focus. Be persistent and you may find yourself on the air.

Your Options Are Limitless

When you are promoting yourself, have a plan and stick to it. At times you will need to step back, regroup, and then proceed with your plan. The options you have to promote yourself are limited only by your imagination. Above all else, network in the community. Be seen. Your only limitations are your expectations.

EXAMPLE: PROMOTIONAL SCHEDULE

Once you have an exhibition, use this form to stay abreast of promotional considerations.

Four Months Prior to Exhibition

_x_ Confirm exhibition details (participants, dates, opening reception, location, etc.).

_x_ Design and print press releases.

_x_ Submit press releases to magazines (longer deadline publications).

Three Months Prior to Exhibition

_x_ Design and be prepared to print invitations.

_x_ Design catalogs, brochures, and other print materials for the exhibition.

Two Months Prior to Exhibition:

_x_ Design and print posters (optional).

One Month Prior to Exhibition

_x_ Print invitations.

_x_ Print catalog, brochure, and other materials.

_x_ Begin soliciting editorial review for your exhibition (dealer involvement).

_x_ Plan details of the opening event (catering, music, VIP arrangements, etc.).

Two Weeks Prior to Exhibition

_x_ Deliver public service announcements to radio and television stations.

_x_ Mail invitations.

_x_ Mail press releases to newspapers, art writers, and art critics (with and without photographs).

_x_ Begin follow-up calls. (You will increase your attendance ten-fold with personal contact.)

_x_ Arrange for a photographer (professional or amateur) to be present at opening.

One Week Prior to Exhibition

_x_ Continue follow-up calls.

Day of Exhibition

_x_ Attend the artist's reception.

Follow Up (Within Two Weeks of Exhibition Closing)

_x_ Send thank-you notes to key patrons of event.

_x_ Update your mailing list with new people and corrected information.

_x_ Follow up personally with those who expressed interest in purchasing your work. (Dealer should be involved.)

_x_ Invite interested people to your gallery or studio.

***EXAMPLE:* PROMOTION CHECKLIST**

To obtain the most from your promotional dollar, it is important to have a plan. Use this worksheet to select the types of promotions you wish to use in your plan. The options are divided into short- and long-term. Select those activities you will begin to use immediately and those you will pursue in the future.

		Today	1 Year	2 Years	Not in Plan
Short-term Promotional Options					
x	Invitations	x			
x	Catalogs	x			
x	Brochures				
x	Tear Sheets				
x	Press Releases—Newspapers	x			
x	Press Releases—Magazines				
x	Public Service Announcements—Television				
x	Public Service Announcements—Radio		x		
x	Editorials/Reviews				
x	Posters			x	
Special Events					
x	Charity Events		x		
x	Open Houses at Your Studio				
x	Demonstrations—Art Fairs/ Public Places				
x	Lectures—Colleges/ Universities			x	
Long-term Promotional Options					
x	Catalogs			x	
x	Newsletters				
x	Videos				
x	Advertising				
x	Articles for Publication				
x	Guest Appearance—Television Shows				x
x	Guest Appearance—Radio Shows				x
x	Books on Your Art				x

Other Promotional Ideas

(Use your imagination about what you can do yourself and the resources available in your community.)

9 PUBLISHING YOUR WORK

QUICK TIP

Publishing can be very profitable and beneficial to your career.

For many artists, the phrase "publishing your art" conjures images of a formidable task from which prints by well-known artists emerge. Most artists do not realize the ease and profitability of the venture. This chapter is provided to dispel the common myths and misunderstandings about publishing fine art and possibly set you on the road to producing limited editions of your own.

What Is Publishing Fine Art?

Let us define publishing fine art as producing a quantity of work based on the multiplication of a piece. These pieces are not necessarily exact copies but are original works referred to as limited editions. Publishing is not confined to the works of the painter or photographer. Sculptors and other artisans can also publish their work by creating additional pieces based upon an original or creating a complete series as limited editions.

Posters are often mistakenly classified as fine art. They are not fine art. Posters are produced by offset printing and are used either for advertising to promote an upcoming event or as decoration.

Artists who decide to publish their work usually do so in conjunction with a publishing company. This arrangement works well for the artist. Publishing companies search for artists whose work they can sell. The artist provides the work, and the publisher produces the editions and uses its established marketing network to sell the pieces. If you are able to join such a venture, I recommend you do so. Be sure you are equitably compensated by the publisher at the final distribution of revenue. Always consult with your attorney before signing any contracts.

Who Can Publish Their Work? When?

Publishing is a viable option for most commercial and fine artists. Publishing is especially beneficial for artists who produce only a few pieces a year. Galleries usually are not interested in their work because such artists do not produce enough to support the gallery's efforts, time, and expenses. Publishing allows these artists to create more work in a short period of time, thereby broadening their market.

Why Publish Your Work?

Publishing your work has many advantages. Beyond the potential financial benefits—granted, earning a living is a noble goal itself—publishing can serve other objectives. Providing works in multiples expands your visibility within the art community. This visibility accelerates the value of your other works as you become more recognized and accessible to more collectors. Publishing can make your work more attractive to a gallery by giving the gallery a broader price range in which to sell your work. As more of your work becomes available, opportunities with additional galleries will arise. The benefits of publishing begin to multiply and gather momentum.

An artist should also consider the size of the original work and what can be hung in a gallery, institution, or home. If your work is large, the number of people who can hang such pieces is limited. For example, the Japanese live in small homes so the art they collect is small, proportional with their homes. Now, for artists who create large pieces, publishers can produce works of a smaller size as multiples of the larger pieces; these are known as "afters." When evaluating your publishing options, consider how your collectors are apt to use the piece.

Some collectors purchase prints rather than paintings, not only for reasons of affordability but also because they believe that the secondary market offers more potential buyers. These collectors view the print as more of a commodity rather than as an original work of art. With numerous prints circulating in the art community, increased visibility of the work enhances the collector's chances for resale. The collector takes advantage of the promotion the gallery or publisher has already done.

Types of Publishing

A wide variety of printing methods are available to the artist who wishes to create limited editions. Common methods are described below.

Serigraphy

More commonly known as silk screen, serigraphy is a printing process in which a medium, such as ink or acrylic, is forced through a fine screen with a squeegee.

Woodcut

Woodcut is a relief printing technique in which the printing surface is carved with special woodcutting tools. The printing medium is then applied directly to the wood and a material such as paper, fabric, glass, or wood is pressed onto the surface.

Etchings

An etching is a type of print made by drawing with a steel etching needle or tool on a highly polished plate. As with the woodcut method, the printing medium is applied directly to the plate and pressed onto a paper or fabric surface.

Lithography

Lithography is a process in which the printing surface has been sensitized by chemical means. The ink picks up the design of the treated areas and is then transferred onto paper or fabric.

Mixed Media

In mixed media, two or more of the above processes are combined. The resulting prints vary slightly from each other. The work is finished by painting or working each print to make it unique and often more desirable. Of the methods listed, the mixed-media approach is the best way to start out if you are on a limited budget.

Iris

The Iris printing process is a process that can reproduce high quality fine art images from digitally stored images or from transparencies. The images are produced on a machine that lays a fine spray of inks on the surface of paper or canvas. This process is an excellent way for artists with limited funds to get started in the fine art publishing business.

QUICK TIP

Keep your editions small and limited, not unlimited.

Other Methods

Some artists are quite creative in designing their own printing techniques. In 1989, we held a David Hockney exhibition at the Modern Museum of Art in Santa Ana, California. At the opening, Hockney arranged for a facsimile machine. He pre-programmed the machine at his studio to send images of his art to the museum. As he arrived for the exhibition, so did his art. The pages were then pinned on the walls, becoming the exhibition. It was quite a media extravaganza!

Hockney later stated he was not producing the work to sell because the facsimile image would fade and had no real value. He was intrigued that fine art images could be transferred with this type of technology.

The Cost of Publishing Your Work

Depending on the method you use, the cost of creating limited editions can vary greatly. If you are working within a modest budget, set your creative talents to the task and research various methods of printmaking. If you wish to get hands-on experience in printmaking, many local colleges offer classes at a modest cost.

Review books on printmaking for ideas you can use with your own work. Remember, however, that offset lithography is not a fine art printing process. It is a photo-mechanical process of printing used for posters, greeting cards, books, magazines, and other mass-produced publications. I strongly recommend not using offset lithography for fine art limited editions.

What Artworks Can Be Published?

As the artist, you must choose the best piece to publish. A painter, for example, will want to select a piece that reproduces well. A sculptor may select a small piece so the cost of multiplying the art does not price the edition out of the targeted marketplace. If you are not sure which piece to publish, seek the advice of art professionals. Artists who work with large pieces will want to consider reducing the physical size of the multiples.

What Size Edition Is Best?

It is my opinion that you should begin with low numbers in your edition. Small editions are generally within the budget and marketing capabilities of the average artist. If you are after the more commercial side of the market, consider producing your edition in series of two or four similar images. People often collect pieces in pairs.

When you publish your work, you have total control over pricing, medium, edition size, and other factors. It is important to understand that the word "limited" means just that. An edition size of more than 100 prints is not desirable to most collectors. Small numbers also are best for sculpture editions. The cost of producing comes down as the size of the edition gets larger, tempting many artists and publishers with the bottom line. Astute collectors often stay away from large editions.

Edition size is a decision the artist should make, based upon his or her career plan. If your primary interest is about increasing revenue and not about raising the importance of your work, then, by all means, print a large edition.

Marketing Your Prints

Before you produce your limited edition, give a great deal of thought to how to market it. Many artists charge ahead with the creative work and completely neglect developing a marketing plan for the final product. The biggest advantage in a venture with a good publisher is being able to use the publisher's marketing network. Before publishers invest in a project, they will have a complete marketing plan detailing the networks and contacts that will be used to sell the edition as quickly as possible. You should think like publishers think.

If you have a mailing list of potential collectors, offer them the opportunity to purchase on the front end of the edition. Many galleries also offer collectors a prepublication discount if they agree to buy the print before it is actually produced. Taking orders before the print is completed helps raise money to cover the cost of printing.

Once you have produced a limited edition, you need to have a sales and marketing plan to promote the edition.

If you are self-publishing in small editions, an impressive selling tool is a tear sheet. A relatively inexpensive tear sheet can be easily made using a word processor and a color photograph. Print the information on the page and attach the photograph of the work to the page. (See the samples on pages 150 and 151.)

If you are working with a publisher, the publisher will usually handle the promotional materials, distribution, and other marketing activities. The publisher will prepare and mail tear sheets and informational materials on you and your work to potential collectors, dealers, and galleries.

Pricing Your Prints

When establishing the pricing structure for your prints, keep in mind that the gallery must make money on the proposition as well. Establish a wholesale price and a retail price for each edition. The retail price—the price paid by the public—should be at least double the wholesale price—the price the gallery pays you. When you produce smaller numbers, the dealer should be able to raise the retail price of the piece more rapidly.

It is easy to determine the prices of prints by artists who work in a style and medium similar to yours. Look through various art publications for prices. Keep current with the market price for prints. Check with galleries in your area that exhibit works similar to your own. Get the opinions of art professionals. Being well informed will help you properly price your works.

Many artists make the mistake of becoming too greedy, thinking the gallery is making all the money. Keep in mind that the gallery has a much larger overhead than does the artist and it is also incurring the expense of marketing the works. To be successful, you have to work closely and cooperatively with the gallery, so choose your gallery representation with care.

Price your prints so both you and the gallery can make a reasonable profit. Don't under-price. An artist I worked with published an edition of 100 serigraph prints. He planned to sell the prints at a wholesale price of $30 and at a suggested retail gallery price of $60. Unfortunately, at this price his prints were not of interest to most fine art galleries because the price did not provide enough profit for the gallery. And if a gallery doesn't profit, the artist doesn't profit.

Sample Price Schedules

For each of your limited editions, you need to establish wholesale and retail price schedules. The price schedule should gradually rise as the supply of prints available for sale diminishes. The rationale is that as available stock decreases, the value of the remaining stock increases so the price goes up. This price structure creates a sense of urgency and is also an incentive to collectors to purchase on the front end of the edition. If you are working with a publisher, the publisher will structure the price schedule.

EXAMPLE: PRICE SCHEDULE STRUCTURES

Example: Increase the price 20 percent after the sale of each 25 percent of the edition.

Edition Size *100*

Number of Prints Sold	Wholesale	Retail
1 to 25 prints	$ 200.00	$ 400.00+
26 to 50 prints	$ 240.00	$ 480.00+
51 to 75 prints	$ 288.00	$ 576.00+
76 to 100 prints	$ 345.00	$ 690.00+

Artist's proof: You can print 10 percent of your edition as artist's proofs.

Create a four-tier schedule based upon each tier being 25 percent of the entire edition. Include the cost of printing, promotion, shipping, and any other related expenses.

Cost per Unit to Produce	*$10.00*
Total Cost of Production	*$1000.00*
Edition size	*100*
Tier 1	
Prints	*1 to 25*
Wholesale	*$200.00*
Suggested Retail	*$400.00+*
Tier 2	
Prints	*26 to 50*
Wholesale	*$240.00*
Suggested Retail	*$480.00+*
Tier 3	
Prints	*51 to 75*
Wholesale	*$288.00*
Suggested Retail	*$576.00+*
Tier 4	
Prints	*76 to 100*
Wholesale	*$345.00*
Suggested Retail	*$690.00+*
Net Profit earned from Wholesale Sales	*$26,825.00*
Net Profit Earned from Direct Sales	*$0*
Total Projected Production and Marketing Costs	*$4,000.00*
Projected Total Net Profits:	*$22,825.00*

***EXAMPLE:* TEAR SHEET**

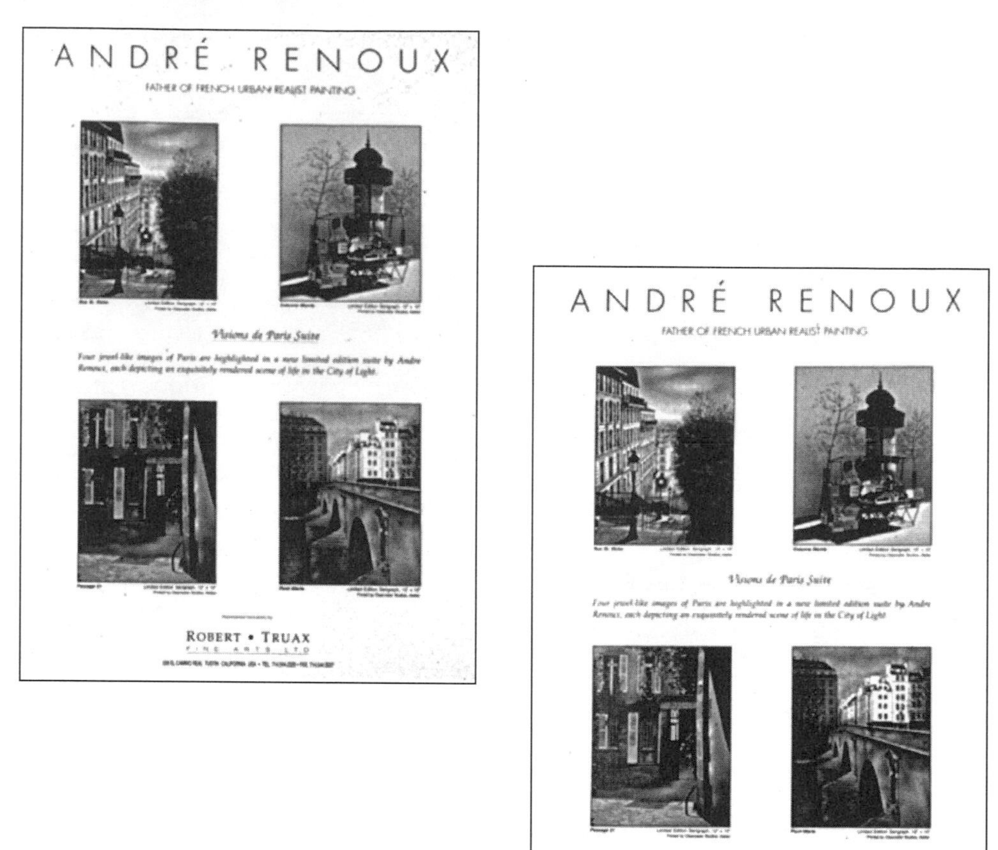

When creating your marketing materials for your limited edition works, print a smaller number of tear sheets with your company or your name, address, and phone on it. (See above left.) Then print the remainder with nothing on the tear sheet. (See above right.)

If you are soliciting galleries, use the tear sheet with your company name printed on the materials, but keep in mind galleries will not want to send clients' materials with your name printed on them. Provide each gallery that purchases your prints a number of blank tear sheets that the gallery can put its name on and send to their clients.

When you create a name for your publishing company, you may wish to create a name that gives the impression that you, the artist, have no connection to the company. This implies that you are an artist that is already handled by a publisher.

ANVIL IRON
PUBLISHING

1945 Sycamore Terrace, Santa Ana, California 98721 ((714) 555-2984 Fax (714) 555-2982

***EXAMPLE:* TEAR SHEET**

JEROME GASTALDI

Gastaldi's works deal with the issue that we are subjected to good as well as negative information and we should question the direct as well as the subliminal.

Black and White

Mixed Media: Serigraph, Lithography, and Hand Worked on 100 percent Museum Rag

24" × 48"

Total edition limited to sixteen numbered prints.

Completion in 1997

FACT
PUBLISHING

FACT PUBLISHING, 30812 PACIFIC COAST HIGHWAY, LAGUNA BEACH, CALIFORNIA 92677
(714) 499-8300

EXAMPLE: PUBLISHING AGREEMENT

This agreement was provided to one of our clients by a publishing company. I recommend that you have a lawyer look at any agreement a publishing company asks you to sign. If you choose not to do so, make certain that you can cancel the agreement if the publishing company does not perform.

This is an agreement between *Bill Smith* (Artist) and *XYZ Publishing Company*, (A New York Corporation).

The company will assume all costs for the publishing and distribution of all Artist's fine art reproductions, including sales and promotion. The Artist shall submit Artist's original art *27 4" × 5" Color Transparencies* (paintings, sculpture, other) and the Company shall select which one(s) the Company will reproduce and distribute. Artist will not permit anyone else to reproduce any of Artist's original art during the period of this agreement.

The Company has the right to sell and promote Artist's reproductions through its network of dealers and in any other way it deems appropriate. Artist will, however, be consulted before decisions are made regarding sale, promotion, image size, and edition size whenever feasible.

The Company and Artist agree to keep confidential the terms of this Agreement, information related to the performance thereof, the business practices and marketing strategies, as well as concepts. This obligation shall survive the terms of this agreement.

The Company agrees to pay the Artist ten (10) percent of the gross sales of each reproduction. Payment will be made each month based upon the gross sales for the prior month. Artist will receive, at no charge, twenty-five artist's proofs of each original reproduced.

This agreement will remain in effect for *five (5)* years from the date of the official release of the first reproduction. If no written notice is given by either party *ninety (90)* days prior to the end of the fifth year, the agreement will automatically be renewed by an additional *five (5)* years.

This agreement, together with all its benefits and obligations, shall be assignable by the Company, but Artist's services are unique and special and are not assignable.

This agreement constitutes the entire agreement between Artist and the Company and no verbal terms, other than as set forth herein, will be considered a part of the agreement between the parties.

XYZ Publishing (Company):

Art Sullivan	*5/22/97*
Signature	Date

Artist/Client:

Bill Smith	*5/27/97*
Signature	Date

An Experience in Self-Publishing

Prior to a scheduled showing of my work, the opportunity arose to publish a print. My dealer thought it a good idea because we could offer something at an affordable price, thereby broadening the range of collectors of my work. An unknown artist at the time, I felt it unlikely that any publisher would take a chance on my work. I decided to publish the print myself.

I produced mixed-media serigraphs with handwork on each piece. The edition of sixteen pieces without proofs was smaller than most printers were interested in producing because they could not make the money they would with a larger project. Eventually, I found a small print studio that agreed to do the print with me.

I worked with the printer on every aspect of the piece: design, color, pulling of each pass of the squeegee. I finished each print with considerable handwork. In retrospect, my mistake was that I had not fully evaluated the complete costs. I could have completed an edition twice the size, stayed within my budget, and still have produced a reasonably sized edition.

This limited edition was still a good decision even though it was not as profitable as it could have been. That first edition, however, enabled me to do a much larger edition a few months later. The owners of a fine art publication purchased one of the first prints and approached me with a proposal to use one of my images on the cover of their publication if I would do a new edition. The owners also offered to market the first 25 percent of my next edition through their distribution network. I took them up on their offer.

Knowing the costs I had just incurred, I did not want to fund a larger edition on my own. I approached a printer with a proposal to joint venture the edition. We split costs and ownership of the edition. The printer had proper shipping and storage facilities; something I did not want to invest in at the time.

Getting a Contract with a Publisher

Getting a contract with a reputable publisher requires the same tenacity as obtaining representation in a gallery or institution. You must determine if the publisher is capable of producing and selling your editions, the manner in which the publisher will market the editions, and if the publisher will be fair and equitable in the distribution of profits.

Because of these considerations, it is imperative that you qualify the publisher. What other artists has the company published? How does your work relate to the publisher's focus? When you feel you have identified a suitable publisher, use the presentation materials and methods you developed in the earlier chapters to introduce yourself. The same rules of presentation apply to the publisher as to any other venue. Never send a package to an unsolicited target.

The primary goal in publishing your art is to encourage people to see and buy your artwork. Associating with a reputable publisher increases your chances for success as opposed to marketing a limited edition yourself. A qualified publisher will know if your work is marketable within the existing network.

Each publisher will have advantages and disadvantages for the goals you have set. One publisher may be perfect in giving you the initial exposure and recognition you need to lead you to your next goal. Consider all the options. Publishers have their own goals. In the process of qualifying publishers, you will learn about the focus of each.

Select a publisher with care. An artist who came to me recently for consultation was having an unfortunate experience with a publisher. At the time we spoke, she was in court trying to obtain the royalties due her. She had signed a contract that allowed the publisher to purchase and publish her work. As compensation, she was to receive continuous royalties from the sales.

The publisher sold nearly $1 million of her prints. Unfortunately, the company declared bankruptcy, and did not pay her royalties. The company dumped the artist's prints on the market, resulting in an instant crash in the value of her limited edition pieces. As you can see, you must be very careful in selecting your publisher, because publishers can do as much, or more, damage to your reputation and financial health as they can benefit it.

Be wary of publishers who approach you with exclusive contracts or promises of mass printing. Have a lawyer review all contracts before signing. Make sure the contract includes a performance/cancellation clause beneficial to you. Have all your questions answered and fully understand the situation before entering into an agreement with a publisher.

Finding a publisher is like finding a gallery—it is important to find one that has good contacts. The publisher will be able to connect you with galleries that will sell not only your editions but also your original art. The evidence is overwhelming—art careers advance through associations.

10 PRICING YOUR WORK

Setting prices for your original work requires the same careful analysis as setting prices for limited edition copies. Setting prices requires thorough research of targeted markets and the artists who are selling in those markets. Compare apples to apples. Look at successful artists who are similar to you in style, medium, and importance. Don't overprice your work by using a blue chip artist's sales prices, unless you also are a blue chip artist.

QUICK TIP

Don't price yourself out of the market.

How do you find this information? Begin by using art publications to identify the artists you want to investigate. Ask the key questions to find out about other artists' backgrounds, importance, and prices.

You may need to visit some of the venues. Ask for materials about the artists and a price sheet for the gallery. Talk with the representative at the gallery. He or she may provide pricing information of other artists. People love to give opinions and display their knowledge about art and artists. If you are preparing for your first show, price your work by comparing it aesthetically to other pieces. Additionally, take into consideration your financial needs.

Developing a Pricing Structure

Armed with the above information, you are ready to price your work. If you have already sold some pieces, the first step is to look at the prices you received. Did those prices meet with resistance? Did all the buyers object or only a few? Are the buyers who objected the ones you are targeting now? If not, do not attach too much importance to their objections.

List all pieces you have sold, the offering price, and the sale price. Were the pieces sold from your studio, through a representative, at a gallery, or at another venue? Has the price of your work increased, decreased, or remained the same?

Next, look at selling prices for pieces similar to yours and then set your prices based on all the information. Also listen to suggestions from your gallery or dealer. Remember, you make the final decisions, but be realistic as to the prices you can reasonably expect.

Be Consistent with Your Prices

If you offer a piece through your gallery, maintain the same price if you also offer it outside the gallery. The quickest way to lose gallery representation and all but destroy your chances for future representation is to undercut the gallery's prices. You must work with your venues, not compete with them.

Further, when represented by galleries in different cities, be consistent and offer your work to each gallery at similar prices. Dealers talk to each other, and if you charge one dealer a significantly greater price for a piece, you will damage your relationship with both. One will view you as biased, the other will view you as dishonest. Protect your business reputation.

I live in a Southern California art community and have many friends who are artists, dealers, and gallery owners. I assure you it is common knowledge which artists sell work from their studios for less than a gallery's retail price. Galleries will not represent artists who sabotage their efforts.

Don't Be Greedy—But Don't Undervalue Yourself

QUICK TIP

If the gallery makes money, you will make money.

I have found it helpful to ask someone whose judgment I trust to review my prices. This review avoids over- or under-valuing the work. I have seen numerous artists grossly inflate the value of their works after experiencing a bit of success. Do not become a legend in your own mind. Setting your original prices too high and then lowering them can be perceived negatively by some. Also, the higher the prices, the smaller the market and the fewer the collectors. A good dealer will help you price your work fairly.

It's appropriate to raise prices for your works after successes, such as being included in an important collection, picked up by a prestigious gallery, or exhibited by or selected for the collection of a museum. Such successes elevate the value of your work. Still, be conservative. You may find the market was receptive to your work, but if you dramatically raise prices, you may lose that market. My advice is to use discretion and not be greedy. The law of supply and demand applies to art as it does to all other commodities.

Sometimes artists become disgruntled with galleries when they see gallery owners taking large cuts from sales revenues. Keep in mind that a gallery has a larger overhead than an artist. The gallery must pay for the cost of displaying and marketing the artworks. The gallery needs to make a fair profit. Traditionally, a fifty-fifty split is fair to the gallery owner and artist.

Pricing is critical to success and cannot be over emphasized. Do not undervalue your work. Collectors will wonder what is wrong with a work if the artist does not value it highly. Keep in mind who your buyers are and what they are willing to pay. Know the market value of your work and that of artists whose work is similar to yours.

Keep an Accurate Record of Your Sales

Maintain a record of all sales of your work, and watch for trends in buying and in the value of your art. Examine the records to see if certain venues sell more at different times of the year. For example, a venue located in a popular ski resort will probably have higher sales during the winter. Knowledge is power—the power for you to get the most from your work.

EXAMPLE: SALES RECORD

Title of Piece	*Red Tree*	**Date of sale**	*Nov. 1997*
Sold By	*Pacific Gallery*	**Venue Type**	*G/D/I*
Contact Name	*Fred Jones*	**Time Listed**	
Address	*124 Hathaway*		
City, State, ZIP	*San Diego, CA 92846*		
Telephone	*(619) 555-9462*		
Facsimile	*(619) 555-5761*		
Sold To	*Ruth Black*	**Collector Type**	*Contemporary*
Address	*4763 Monrovia Pl.*		
City, State, ZIP	*La Jolla, CA 94361*		
Telephone	*(619) 555-9482*		
Facsimile	*(619) 555-2901*		
Listed Price	*$2,000.00*	**Sold for**	*$1,900.00*
Net Monies Received	*$950.00*	**Monies paid venue**	*$950.00*

Title of Piece		**Date of sale**	
Sold By		**Venue Type**	
Contact Name		**Time Listed**	
Address			
City, State, ZIP			
Telephone			
Facsimile			
Sold To		**Collector Type**	
Address			
City, State, ZIP			
Telephone			
Facsimile			
Listed Price		**Sold for**	
Net Monies Received		**Monies paid venue**	

QUICK TIP

Don't wait—get going now!

Getting Started

Perhaps the most uncomfortable and frustrating activity for artists is approaching the business world of galleries, museums, and other venues with their work. They often have doubts: Is my work good enough? Will they understand my art? Do my materials reflect what I want to say? What if they reject me? These and other fears can be conquered.

Over the past few years, *Art & Reality* has been used to clear away these stumbling blocks. Both entry level and established artists have used the guidelines in this book to find success and advance their careers and knowledge.

If you read the chapter "Presenting Your Work," you will know the importance of having a strong, cohesive body of work to show. Once developed, it's time to create a presentation that convinces the art world of your talent.

Keep in mind success means different things to different artists. Many artists are already financially successful but seek representation or exposure in other areas. Some artists have achieved gallery success but have never had academic exhibitions. This book helps artists to identify goals and provides artists with methods of achieving these goals in the shortest time possible.

Now with your presentation materials in order, turn to page 87 and review the checklist. Double-check your materials. Only when you are truly satisfied your materials are cohesive, focused, and representative of your best work should you proceed. That first impression must be the best impression.

Fine Art Communication Technologies, Inc., provides services to artists who do not wish to personally market their careers. The staff uses the same forms and materials provided in this book. Even so, we encourage all artists striving to develop or expand their careers to become actively involved in marketing themselves and their work.

You will find that presenting your work—especially after the first few experiences—becomes a comfortable process. After a few successes, presenting your work becomes quite easy.

If your work appeals to a more commercial market, results will likely come faster than for those pursuing academic venues. In either case, however, you must follow a plan. The key to success is keep presenting your work.

I suggest an artist make at least four qualified presentations per month. You may find it convenient to send out all your presentations the first week or two of each month, as you need the next two weeks to follow up. When first promoting yourself as an artist, you may want to send out more than four presentations, but if you have qualified the venues, four presentations should be sufficient. (Note: Many galleries will tell you to send slides, but we recommend a complete presentation.) The most important thing is to be persistent.

First Week

- Qualify your targets.
- Make a list of your targets.
- Telephone the venue or visit it in person.
- Review your presentation checklist.

I recommend sending out all four of your presentation packages during the first week, which gives you three weeks to concentrate on follow up and preparing new packages for the next month. If you are more comfortable with staggering your presentations, do so. The important thing is to continue approaching four venues each month until you achieve your desired results.

Second Week

- Start follow up. Within a few days of sending the package, contact your prospects to confirm receipt of your materials.
- If possible, begin a dialog with your prospects.

If you approach galleries with hopes of having a solo show and you are offered a group exhibition, I urge you to accept the offer. A group exhibition still provides you with and demonstrates visibility to the gallery that your work will sell to its clientele. If you have approached institutions, seek inclusion in future exhibitions. Do your homework. In either case, what you want most is an opportunity to show your work.

Third Week

- Continue follow up.
- Ask the venues if they reached a decision or have additional questions about your work.
- If the venues show no interest by now, ask for the return of your materials. If a venue wishes to continue reviewing your materials, let it. Some venues need more time to make a decision.

Fourth Week

- Continue follow up.
- If you have had no further indication of interest in your work, request the return of your materials.
- Be polite. A venue's policies and interest may change, so keep the door open.
- Start preparing for the next four-week period.

Continue monthly contacts, review each venue approached, and continue to improve. Each time you make a presentation, it gets easier. Stay focused and keep presenting until you have enough representation to meet your needs. All your goals are within your reach.

EXAMPLE: PRESENTATION SCHEDULE

First Week or Monthly Presentations

Venue	Contact	Address	Phone
Marton Gallery	*Joseph*	*1254 Gold St., Los Angeles, CA 90001*	*(213) 555-0890*
BC Gallery	*Bill*	*752 J Ave., Long Beach, CA 90801*	*(310) 555-0051*
Mach Gallery	*Ann*	*4763 Nyber Pl., La Jolla, CA 92343*	*(619) 555-9621*
Oliver Gallery	*Susan*	*9786 Josh St., Costa Mesa, CA 92656*	*(714) 555-8624*

Second Week

Venue	Contact	Response
Oliver Gallery	*Susan*	*Interested. Will call next week.*

Third Week

Venue	Contact	Response
Martha Mack Gallery	*Ann*	*Not interested. Will return materials.*
William Mortan Gallery	*Joseph*	*Needs more time to review materials.*

Fourth Week

Venue	Contact	Response
BC Gallery	*Bill*	*Interested in using work in spring show.*

11 FINDING FUNDING FOR YOUR WORK

As part of developing your career plan, consider the support available to artists through grants, artist-in-residency programs, and sponsorships. Grants and programs for the visual arts are available for all types of work and all types of artists. These programs can be used to obtain financial support and time to develop your work and career. Both you and the sponsoring organization benefit from these opportunities.

QUICK TIP

Keep your eyes, ears, and mind open. There are many opportunities.

What Is a Grant?

A grant is an award of cash or provision of materials based upon a given set of criteria. These criteria are determined by the sponsoring organization and are based upon the focus of the organization's efforts. For example, one artist I work with obtained funding to develop a traveling exhibition of works based upon art created by the institutionalized mentally ill. For the artist, it was an opportunity to support an issue he felt strongly about and to be financially supported for the efforts. For the sponsoring organization, it was an opportunity to educate the public about this social issue. Both parties benefited.

What Is an Artist-in-Residency Program?

An artist-in-residency program is a form of grant designed to provide artists with the opportunity to live and work in an environment conducive to artistic development. The artist may be given a place to live, work, and exhibit over a prescribed length of time. Funds include financial support to the artist during the time of residency. On occasion, part of the residency program will involve teaching or lecturing on the part of the artist.

What Are Sponsorships?

Sponsorships are projects funded by individuals, organizations, and corporations, again usually based upon the focus of their efforts or products. For example, an artist who works with photography may obtain a sponsorship from a company involved with photographic supplies or processing. The opportunities for these kinds of sponsorships are prevalent.

Who Qualifies?

You do! Once again, the qualifications for a grant are established by the sponsoring organization and may include things such as birthplace, heritage, experience, age, sex, style of art, subject matter, project, religious affiliation, financial need, and the like. It will be your job to search through the grant resources to find those programs that interest you and for which you might be qualified.

Many artists are intimidated by the idea of applying for grants. They are overwhelmed by the prospect of filling out applications, submitting materials, and possibly being interviewed. You need not be. The techniques for presenting to potential venues that you have learned and put into practice through this book apply just the same when approaching foundations and organizations for grants.

How Are Grants Awarded?

The actual award process is determined by the sponsoring organization but generally involves these steps: The artist submits an application along with his or her presentation materials. These materials are preliminarily reviewed by a selected jury of individuals from the sponsoring organization or the community. Preliminary finalists are then selected. Usually a number of reviews take place. Artists may be asked to present works in person or be interviewed by a jury. The grant is then awarded to the winner.

How Do You Apply for a Grant?

The entire process of applying for a grant is similar to what you do each day in advancing your career.

Grant Research—aka Market Research

The first step is to investigate what grant opportunities are available to you specifically. Read through the various grant resource books that you can find at bookstores and in university, college, and public libraries. Identify those grants whose criteria you meet. Do not spend the time to apply for a grant if you do not qualify. A number of grant resource listings have been provided in the appendix of this book.

Investigate the Selected Grants

Research each of the specific grants you have selected. Begin by calling or writing for the application forms and any additional information the organization can provide about the grant or itself. The more you know and understand the funding organization, the more clear and focused a presentation you will be able to make. You may even ask for a list of the artists who have been awarded the grant in the past, including any visual or contact materials the organization may be able to provide. This book provides two worksheets to help you investigate each grant as fully as possible. Be sure to note the deadline for applying for a grant.

Develop Your Concept and Proposal

After reading the materials you have collected and before you begin filling out the grant application forms, develop a proposal or focus for your presentation. Depending upon the criteria for the grant, develop a concept of how your art will be used or developed in conjunction with the award. For example, if the grant involves an environmental issue, how will your art enhance the public's awareness of this issue? Will your art inform the public? Will it intensify emotions or awareness? What are your ideas for this "marriage" of your art with the organization's objectives?

Unless otherwise instructed by the grant application, this proposal is for you to use to focus your answers on the application. If you have a directed goal, your application will reflect that. Conversely, if you are indecisive and do not clearly present your concept to the organization, your lack of a goal will be obvious.

Completing the Grant Application

Many artists have difficulty completing the application. But now that you understand the grant, the organization, and your concept for the project, completing the application will be much easier. Be sure that your writing is academic and simple, concise, and direct. Such writing is far more effective than rambling or flowery prose.

Start by making a few copies of the application to use for your rough drafts. Set the original forms aside so they do not become soiled. Read the application thoroughly before answering any questions. Then go back to the beginning and answer each and every question asked on the form. You may wish to use language similar to that used by the organization in its own informational materials. The terminology an organization uses to describe itself can give you a great deal of information.

When you have completed a rough draft of the application and any required essay, have the application read over by someone, preferably someone who has an understanding of art, the art community, and the focus of the grant. After this first review, continue editing the draft until you are confident about what you have written.

Once all writing has been finished, type or laser print the answers onto the original application forms. At no time should you handwrite a grant application. It is important for you to present yourself as a professional, just as you would with any presentation. Proofread the final application for typos and errors, and make all needed corrections. Photocopy the completed application for your records.

Submit the cover letter, application forms, and presentation package to the organization as stated in the instructions. Use a clean padded envelope to submit your package. Remember, as always, to clearly address the package and affix sufficient postage.

Follow-up

If possible, stay in contact with the grant committee or the organization that is sponsoring the grant. Call the organization to confirm receipt of your package. When the various key dates of the selection process arrive, contact the group for information to determine if you have been selected as a finalist. Remember, though, do not be pushy.

Other Opportunities

In addition to grants, residency programs, and sponsorships, numerous other sources for funding your work are available. Some of these resources are listed in funding resource books. Also investigate resources in your community. If your work could be closely linked with a business or organization, you might be able to persuade the business or organization to support one of your projects.

For example, many nonprofit organizations look for artists who can help them develop community projects. One artist I work with also produces videos. She used her talents to produce a 15-minute production for the benefit of a struggling nonprofit group. The funding for the materials and her time were donated by a benefactor to the organization. She now has an impressive video as part of her portfolio, and the nonprofit organization has raised $500,000 for a new building. Again, both parties benefited.

EXAMPLE: TELEPHONE RESEARCH WORKSHEET: FUNDING OPPORTUNITIES

Date of Contact *4/19/97*

Source of Listing *Art in America*

Referred by ______

Name of Funding *Artist-in-Residence Program*

Name of Sponsoring Organization *Tulsa Oklahoma Cultural Center*

Address *P.O. Box 519 Spruce*

City, State, ZIP *Tulsa, OK 73421*

Country *USA*

Telephone *(918) 555-5130*

Facsimile *(918) 555-8234*

Owner/Director *Elizabeth Whitlock*

Title *Director*

Spoke with *Josh*

Department *Sales*

Date Funding Application is Due *2/7/97*

Type of Funding?

____ Grant

_x_ Artist-in-Residency

____ Sponsorship

____ Other ______________

Funding Criteria?

Must be a resident of Oklahoma and a full-time working artist.

Do you meet all the required criteria? Yes _x_ No ___

If "No," should you still pursue applying for this award? Yes ___ No _x_

Maximum Award Amount *$5,000.00*

What other items are awarded? (housing, studio, exhibition space, teaching, etc.)

Housing and the use of an auto.

What are the terms of the award?

Two weeks teaching at the cultural center.

What materials are requested to be presented and how?

Supplied by the center.

What is the purpose of the award?

To allow the regional artist the opportunity to work with a full-time working artist.

What is the focus of the sponsoring organization?

Support of regional artists.

What are your feelings about the organization's focus, beliefs, products, and activities?

Great concept. They help many struggling artists.

Name the artists who have received funding in prior years.

Jasper Slavich, Sandra Duley

You may wish to call the artists who have been awarded a grant in prior years to ask questions about the organization, application process, their presentation, and other aspects of the grant.

Comments

I spoke with Sandra Duley and she said it was a great experience. The people at the center treated her very well, and the grant opened up other opportunities for her.

EXAMPLE: APPLICATION TRACKING WORKSHEET

Name of Funder	*Fine Arts Foundation*
Name of Sponsoring Organization	*Hazel Grans Fine Artist Trust*
Telephone	*(310) 555-0864*
Application Due	*8/1/96*
Application Submitted	*7/15/96*
Confirmation of Receipt	*7/20/96*
First Review Cut	*Considered*
Second Review Cut	*Considered*
Third Review Cut	*Considered*
Fourth Review Cut	*Considered*
Final Decision	*?*
Appointment for Presentation	*12/1/97*
Appointment for Interview	
Final Outcome	

Notes and images from application (Remember to retain a copy of the completed application for your records):

EPILOGUE

Over the years I have had the opportunity to meet many artists—some are successful and many could be. I do feel that besides having talent and a desire to create art, making a commitment to pursue a career as an artist can be one of the most fulfilling decisions a person can make in his or her life. Whether you are a full-time artist or have to support your passion with another job, what is important is never to stop creating. The ability to create is a marvelous gift.

If you have the desire to let other people into your world of creation, then follow your desire, use the simple guidelines in this book, and pursue your goals. Other than God's creations, artists make everything else in life worth looking at.

APPENDIX

The following references and organizations will help you research information and opportunities to build your career.

ART LAW/ACCOUNTING

These organizations and publications will help you understand your legal and financial responsibilities as a professional artist. For example, in working with contracts, it is important for you to have proper legal advice so that you are properly protected and fully understand what you are obligating yourself to.

ORGANIZATIONS

American Council for the Arts
1 East 53rd St.
New York, NY 10022

Artists for Tax Equity
Graphic Artists Guild
11 West 20th St., 8th Floor
New York, NY 10011

Volunteer Lawyers for the Arts
1 East 53rd St.
New York, NY 10022

PUBLICATIONS

The Artists Friendly Legal Guide
by F. Conner, R. Gilcrest,
P. Karlen, J. Perwin & D. Spatt
Cincinnati: North Light Books
1507 Dana Ave.
Cincinnati, OH 45207
revised: 1988

Business and Legal Forms for Fine Artists
by Tad Crawford
New York: Allworth Press
revised: 1990

The Business of Art
by Lee Caplin
New York: Prentice Hall
revised: 1991

The Business of Being an Artist
by Daniel Grant
New York: Allworth Press

Legal Guide for the Visual Artist
by Tad Crawford
New York: Allworth Press
revised: 1989

Art Organizations

The purpose of art organizations is to support artists and enhance community awareness of the arts. The organizations listed below will serve as starting points for your research. You will find other groups in your local area that may also interest you.

American Association of Museums
1575 I St., NW, Suite 400
Washington, DC 20007

American Council for the Arts
1 East 53rd St.
New York, NY 10022

American Craft Council
72 Spring St.
New York, NY 10012

Artist Equity Association
PO Box 28068
Central Station
Washington, DC 20038

Artists Consortium Library
1 East 53rd St.
New York, NY 10022

Association of Independent Film and Video Makers
625 Broadway, 9th Floor
New York, NY 10012

Deaf Artists of America
302 N. Goodman St., Suite 205
Rochester, NY 14607

Graphic Artists Guild
11 West 20th St.
New York, NY 10011

National Alliance of Media Arts and Culture
655 13th St., Suite 201
Oakland, CA 94612

National Assembly of Local Art Agencies
927 15th St. NW, 12th Floor
Washington, DC 20005

National Assembly of State Arts Agencies
1010 Vermont Ave., NW, Suite 920
Washington, DC 20005

National Association of Artists Organizations
918 F St. NW
Washington, DC 20004

National Center on the Arts and Aging
National Council on the Aging
409 3rd St., SW, Suite 200
Washington, DC 20024

National Endowment for the Arts
1100 Pennsylvania Ave., NW
Washington, DC 20506

Visual AIDS
155 Avenue of the Americas
New York, NY 10013

Copyright Registration

Copyrighting your work and your presentation materials, such as catalogs and brochures, is an important aspect of being a professional artist. You put a great deal of effort into your works and it is in your best interest to protect them. The following guides will help you protect your works:

Copyright Information Kit
Copyright Office
Library of Congress
Washington, D.C. 20540

How to Protect Your Creative Work
by David A. Weinstein
John Wiley and Sons
605 Third Ave.
New York, NY 10158

VLA Guide to Copyright for the Visual Arts
Volunteer Lawyers of the Arts
1 East 53rd St.
New York, NY 10022

Employment and Career Opportunities

Many organizations and publications can help the artist find employment and career opportunities within the arts. These sources stay current with opportunities at local, regional, and national levels.

Art Calendar
PO Box 199
Upper Fairmount, MD 21867

AVISO
American Association of Museums
1575 I St., NW, Suite 400
Washington, D.C. 20005

Arts in Education Program
Office of Public Partnership
National Endowment for the Arts
1100 Pennsylvania Ave., NW
Washington, DC 20506

For the Working Artist: A Survival Guide
by Judith Luther
National Network for Artist Placement
935 W. Avenue 37
Los Angeles, CA 90065

National Art Education Association
1916 Association Dr.
Reston, VA 22091

National Directory of Arts Internships
by Warren Christensen
National Network for Artist Placement
935 West Avenue 37
Los Angeles, CA 90065

National Guild of Community Schools of the Arts
40 N. Van Brunt St.
Englewood, NJ 07631

Fine Art Printing

Finding the right publisher is as important as finding the right dealer to represent your work. The following guide will start you off in the right track:

Directory of Art Publishers, Book Publishers and Record Companies
Directors Guild Publishers and The Consultant Press
18757 Wildflower Dr.
Penn Valley, CA 95946

Gallery Directories/Dealers

Targeting the right galleries and dealers for your work is an important part of developing your career. Qualifying the venue before you present will save you time, money and frustration. The following organizations and publications will help you begin your search:

American Art Directory
by R.R. Bowker
New York, NY

American Art Galleries: The Illustrated Guide to Their Art & Artists
Facts on File
11 Penn Plaza
New York, NY 10001

Art & Auction International Directory
Art & Auction
440 Park Avenue South, 14th Floor
New York, NY 10016

Art Diary: The World's Art Directory
Milan, Italy: Giancardo Politi Editore
Distributed Art Publishers
636 Broadway, 12th Floor
New York, NY 10012

Art in America Annual Guide to Galleries, Museums and Artists
Art in America
575 Broadway
New York, NY 10012

Directory of Fine Art Representatives and Corporate Art Collections
Directors Guild Publishers and The Consultant Press
18757 Wildflower Dr.
Penn Valley, CA 95946

Directory of Galleries for the Fine Artist
Directors Guild Publishers and The Consultant Press
18757 Wildflower Dr.
Penn Valley, CA 95946

International Directory of Corporate Art Collections
ArtNews and International Art Alliance
New York, NY
revised: 1989

International Directory of the Arts
Gale Research, Inc.
835 Penobscot Bldg.
Detroit, MI 48226

The Visual Arts Handbook
Visual Arts Ontario
439 Wellington St.
Toronto, Ontario, Canada M5V 1E7

Grant and Funding Opportunities

Grants and programs for the visual arts are available for all types of work and all types of artists. These programs can be used to obtain financial support and time to develop your work and career. The following publications will help you begin your research:

Artist Help: The Artist's Guide to Work-related Human & Social Services
by the Research Center for Arts & Culture
Columbia University
Neal-Schuman Publishers
100 Varick St.
New York, NY 10013

Directory of Financial Aid for Women
Reference Service Press
1100 Industrial Rd., Suite 9
San Carlos, CA 94070

Directory of Grants in the Humanities
The Oryx Press
4041 N. Central, Suite 700
Phoenix, AZ 85012

Foundation Grants to Individuals
The Foundation Center
79 Fifth Ave.
New York, NY 10003
Revised: 1991

Guide to Programs and Program Application Guidelines and Forms
Public Information Office
National Endowment for the Arts
1100 Pennsylvania Ave., NW
Washington, DC 20506

Money to Work II - Funding for Visual Artists
Art Resources International with support from the NEA
Edited by Helen M. Brunner and Donald H. Russell, with Grant E. Samuelsen
5813 Nevada Ave., NW
Washington, DC 20015

Money for Visual Artists
by The American Council for the Arts
Edited by Suzanne Niemeyer
New York: Allworth Press

The National Directory of Grants and Aid to Individuals in the Arts
by Nancy A. Fandel
Washington International Arts Letter, 1987
PO Box 12010
Des Moines, IA 50312

The Proposal Writer's Guide
by Michael Burns
Development and Technical Assistance Center
70 Audubon St.
New Haven, CT 06510

Visual Arts Residency: Sponsor Organizations
Mid-Atlantic Arts Foundation
11 E. Chase St., Suite 2A
Baltimore, MD 21202

Magazines

Subscribe to a number of art periodicals. These publications will help you stay on top of what is happening in the art world and what venues may be potential candidates for your work. Select a few of the national or international publications, but don't forget to include those that report on the events and artists of your region and style.

The following list of publications includes most of the major periodicals on art:

American Artist
1515 Broadway
14th Floor
New York, NY 10036

American Association of Museums
1575 I St., NW, #400
Washington, D.C. 20005

Art & Antiques
919 Third Ave.
15th Floor
New York, NY 10022

Art & Artists
280 Broadway St., #412
New York, NY 10007

Art & Auction
440 Park Ave. South
14th Floor
New York, NY 10016

Art Beat
PO Box 123
Mt. Shasta, CA 96067

Art Business News
19 Old Kings Hwy. South
Darien, CT 06820

Art Gallery International
PO Box 52940
Tulsa, OK 74152

Art in America
575 Broadway
New York, NY 10012

Art Now
97 Grayrock Rd., #5541
Clinton, NJ 08809

Art of the West
15612 Highway 7, #235
Minnetonka, MN 55345

Art Papers
PO Box 77348
Atlanta, GA 30357

Art Previews
1200 West 38th St.
Indianapolis, IN 46208

Artforum
65 Bleecker St.
New York, NY 10012

Artist's Magazine
1501 Dana Avenue
Cincinnati, OH 45207

ARTnews
48 West 38th St.
New York, NY 10018

Artscene
PO Box 97
Freeport, NY 11520

ArtSource Quarterly
18757 Wildflower Dr.
Penn Valley, CA 95946

Artspeak
245 8th Ave., #285
New York, NY 10011

ARTWEEK
2149 Paragon Dr., Ste. 100
San Jose, CA 95131

Communication Arts
410 Sherman Ave.
Palo Alto, CA 94306

Corporate Art News
48 West 38th St.
New York, NY 10018

Decor
330 N. Fourth St.
St. Louis, MO 63102

Flash Art
799 Broadway
New York, NY 10003

Graphic Design USA
1556 3rd Ave., Ste. 405
New York, NY 10128

Museum News
1575 I St., NW, #400
Washington, D.C. 20005

Office Museum Directory
3004 Glenview Rd.
Wilmette, IL 60091

Southwest Art
4 High Ridge Park
Stamford, CT 06905

US Art
200 S. 6th St., Ste. 51
Minneapolis, MN 55402

USA Illustrator
500 South 4th St.
Minneapolis, MN 55415

Women Artists News
300 Riverside Dr., #8A
New York, NY 10025

Mailing Lists

Keeping a current mailing list of potential collectors, galleries, museums, institutions, and other venues is an important aspect of your promotional plan. In addition to the people whom you meet in the course of your daily activities, you can also add to your list through quality mail order data bases.

ArtNetwork
18757 Wildflower Dr.
Penn Valley, CA 95946

Direct Marketing Association
1120 Avenue of the Americas
New York, NY 10036

Media Directories

As you begin to contact the press, it is important for you to develop a good list of media contacts. The following guides will help you begin your search:

Magazine Industry Market Place
New York: R.R. Bowker

National Radio Publicity Directory
Peter Glenn Publications, Ltd.
42 West 38th St.
New York, NY 10018

Media Personnel Directory
Detroit: Gales Research Co.

Museum Directories

Targeting the right museums for your work is an important part of developing your career. Qualifying the venue before you present will save you time, money, and frustration. The following publications will help you begin your search:

Art in America Annual Guide to Galleries, Museums and Artists
Art in America
575 Broadway
New York, NY 10012

International Directory of the Arts
Gale Research, Inc.
835 Penobscot Bldg.
Detroit, MI 48226

American Art Directory
R.R. Bowker
121 Chanlon Rd.
New Providence, NJ 07924

Art Diary: The World's Art Directory
Milan, Italy: Giancardo Politi Editore
Flash Art
799 Broadway
New York, NY 10003

The Official Museum Directory
The American Association of Museums
121 Chanlon Rd.
New Providence, NJ 07924

Photography

There are some basic guidelines to follow in photographing your works. The following references provide a good foundation for understanding how to produce a good photo:

Photographing Your Artwork: A Step-By-Step Guide to Taking High Quality Slides at an Affordable Price
by Russell Hart
Cincinnati: North Light Books
1507 Dana Ave.
Cincinnati, OH 45207

Photographing Your Artwork
by Russell Hart
Cincinnati: North Light Books
1507 Dana Ave.
Cincinnati, OH 45207
revised: 1987

Trade Shows/Art Fairs/Juried Competitions

Trade shows and art fairs are a good way for artists to sell their work directly to the public. A number of prestigious and exclusive art shows are held throughout the year. Juried competitions also expose your work to the public, allowing it to be reviewed by critics, curators, art dealers, college professors, art organization directors, and a variety of professionals from the community.

The following guides will help you begin identifying and qualifying those fairs and competitions that are of interest to you:

Art Competition Handbook
by John M. Anglelini
Cincinnati: North Light Books
1507 Dana Ave.
Cincinnati, OH 45207
revised: 1986

Guidebook for Competitions and Commissions
Visual Arts Ontario
439 Wellington St.
Toronto, Ontario, Canada M5V 1E7

GLOSSARY

Academic - In reference to style of presentation, academic materials promote the importance of the art—the historical comparison of the art to other important works and the significance of the artist's progression in development to the art world.

Archive - A complete record of all materials produced relating to an artist's works and career, including any and all printed materials depicting or discussing the artist's work.

Artist's Proof - These prints are provided for the artist to verify color correctness and clarity. In most processes, artist's proofs amount to 10 percent of the edition. The artist's proofs are often signed "A-P" and numbered.

Artist's Statement - A brief declaration by the artist describing his or her work, philosophy, and source of inspiration.

Body of Work - A collection of works that is presented as a single unit. Often, a body of work will have a theme or common thread that links the individual pieces.

Chronological - Organization of items in order of the date each was produced.

Collector - A person who purchases a piece of art. Collectors often follow the career of artists in whom they are interested, purchasing a number of pieces over time.

Commercial - In reference to style of presentation, commercial materials promote the artist to generate revenues; in contrast, academic materials present the art. Commercial tools are often highly polished sales tools.

Commercial Gallery - A commercial gallery is a place of business in which the sole purpose is to sell art for a profit. This type of venue usually focuses on selling "product" as opposed to a gallery that promotes the career of the artist.

Dealer - A person who deals in the sale of art. There are several types of dealers. Some dealers own or direct a gallery. Other dealers are independent and work in conjunction with a gallery dealer.

Exposure - The exhibition or showing of works of art for viewing by persons other than the artist.

Gallery - A place of business in which the primary purpose is to sell art for a profit. Some galleries work exclusively with "product" and others emphasize the development of the artist's career.

Hand-Touched - In reference to limited edition printing, the application of media or manipulation of the print by the artist. The artist's hand has "touched" the work.

Institution - Venues, including museums, universities, and foundations, that focus on the academic value of artwork rather than on its economic value.

Patron - An individual who supports an institution such as a museum. Patrons who purchase works for collections are known as collectors.

Philosophy - The artist's theories and beliefs that influence his or her creativity. Often thought of as the artist's reason for making art. Some artists do not have philosophies but work purely for aesthetic reasons.

Promotion - The process of publicizing artwork, artists, or art events. The purpose of promotion is to heighten the awareness and interest of the public in the artwork.

Publish - The process of producing a quantity of work based on the multiplication or reproduction of a piece. These pieces are not copies but are usually original works unto themselves.

Retail - The price the public pays for a work of art.

Scholarship - In reference to artwork, writings that have been published about artwork.

Strategies - The planned steps an artist takes in the development of his or her career.

Targets - The selected venues to which the artist's works will be presented.

Telephone Research - The process of gathering information over the telephone; used to find and select appropriate venues or individuals.

Venue - Any space used for the exhibition or sale of art.

Wholesale - The price paid by a gallery or intermediary who will in turn sell the work at a greater price to the public.

WORKSHEETS

Now that you are ready to fill out the forms provided in this section, you may wish to make copies of the master forms you will be using most often.

I recommend you purchase a three-ring binder to hold your copies. You will be referring to these forms often.

MARKET SELECTION WORKSHEET

This worksheet lists all the potential markets for your art. The applicability of each venue for the fine arts or the commercial arts should be noted in the two columns to the right.

Rank the priority of each selected venue within your career goals as follows: 1—highest priority, 2—moderate priority, 3—low priority, and 4—would be nice if it fits in. This ranking will establish the order in which you will address the venue as you begin carrying out your plan.

	Market	Order of Priority	Fine Art Venue	Commercial Art Venue
_____	Fine Arts Gallery	_____		
_____	Commercial Gallery	_____		
_____	Gallery Chain	_____		
_____	Co-op Gallery	_____		
_____	Art Dealer	_____		
_____	Independent Art Dealer	_____		
_____	Corporate Art Consultant	_____		
_____	Studio Sales (Caution!)	_____		
_____	Museums	_____		
_____	Museum Sales/Rental Gallery	_____		
_____	Traveling Museum Shows	_____		
_____	Curator for Collections	_____		
_____	Publishing	_____		
_____	Commissions	_____		
_____	Art Fairs and Shows	_____		
_____	Juried Shows and Competitions	_____		
_____	Schools and Universities	_____		
_____	State and County Fairs	_____		
_____	Fund-raisers	_____		
_____	Corporate Loans	_____		
_____	Religious Groups	_____		
_____	Libraries	_____		
_____	Restaurants, Bars, etc.	_____		
_____	Interior Designers	_____		
_____	Trade/Barter	_____		
_____	Internet Site	_____		

PRESENTATION COVER LETTER WORKSHEET

Date ______________________

Name ______________________

Title ______________________

Venue ______________________

Address ______________________

City, State, ZIP ______________________

Dear ______________________

Opening Paragraph

(Remind Phone Call)

____

____

(Presenting Your Art)

____

____

Second Paragraph

(Strength of Your Art)

____

____

(Tie-in Statement)

____

____

____

____

Closing Paragraph

(Call to Action)

____

____

(Your Follow-up Step)

____

____

Sincerely,

(Your Name)

____

PRESENTATION CHECKLIST

- ____ Cover letter
- ____ Essay and artist's statement (optional)
- ____ Catalog, brochure, biography page, presentation binder, CD-ROM, etc.
- ____ Three 8" × 10" or 8-1/2" × 11" color photographs
- ____ One or two 8" × 10" or 8-1/2" × 11" black-and-white photographs
- ____ Nine to twenty properly labeled slides of all pieces shown in the catalog or brochure
- ____ Press releases and promotional materials ready for print (optional). A price list (only if sending to galleries).
- ____ Self-addressed, stamped padded envelope for return of presentation materials

Remaining Archive Materials

- ____ An up-to-date academic résumé (updated throughout your career)
- ____ Letters received from dealers, curators, and others discussing your works (positive or negative)
- ____ Black-and-white installation photographs
- ____ Photographs of important people attending your show
- ____ Invitations to shows/exhibitions
- ____ Press releases regarding shows/exhibitions
- ____ All promotional materials for each show/exhibition
- ____ Newspaper reviews of your works/shows/exhibitions (positive or negative)
- ____ Magazine reviews of your works/shows/exhibitions
- ____ Brochures, tear sheets, etc.
- ____ Other materials about you or your works from the art community

TELEPHONE RESEARCH WORKSHEET: GALLERIES, MUSEUMS, AND OTHER VENUES

Date of Contact ____________________

Source of Listing ____________________

Referred by ____________________

Name of Museum ____________________

Affiliation ____________________

Goal of this call

Piece in Group Show ____ **Solo Show** ____

Representation ____ **Acquire for Collection** ____

Address ____________________

City, State, ZIP ____________________

Country ____________________

Telephone ____________________

Facsimile ____________________

E-mail ____________________

Director ____________________

Curator ____________________

Spoke with ____________________

Title ____________________

Hours ____________________

What types of art are exhibited? ____________________

What is the museum's focus? ____________________

Do they show contemporary or traditional artists?

Contemporary ____ Traditional ____

What type of artists do they show?

Local ____ Regional ____

National ____ International ____

What artists are in their collection? ____________________

Is my work appropriate for this space? Yes ____ No ____

What are their presentation policies? ____________________

____

Other? ____________________

PRESENTATION TRACKING WORKSHEET

Once you have organized and completed your presentation packages, you are ready to begin qualifying and presenting your work to targeted venues. Use this worksheet to track the sequence of steps within each presentation.

Contact Venue: ____________________

Action	Date Completed
Telephone research call. Initial introduction of artist to the qualified venue.	_________
Personally present or mail the complete presentation package, including a personalized cover letter reflecting the key points discussed in the initial conversation.	_________
Within at least four days of the presentation, call the package recipient to make sure the package was received (if mailed) and to determine if the recipient has had an opportunity to review your materials.	_________
Send the appropriate follow-up letter as described in the chapter "Written Communications."	_________
Continue to follow up with the venue, calling and sending correspondence until receiving a final answer, either positive or negative. Remember, however, not to be overly pushy. Simply stay in regular contact with the venue.	_________
If the venue makes a commitment, send a letter confirming all the terms of the agreement for exhibition, representation, or other activity. You may decide to allow the venue to keep your presentation package for sales and promotional purposes or you may allow the venue to keep the catalog and return the other materials for future presentations.	_________
Send a thank-you note for the venue's time and efforts in reviewing your work. You may request your materials be returned, offering to let the venue keep your catalog for future reference.	_________
If a certain amount of interest was expressed in your work but no commitment was made at this time, place this venue on your mailing list. Send regular notes, articles, invitations, and the like to your contact to keep the venue abreast of the progress your career is making. Above all else, actively work your mailing list.	_________

PRESENTATION LOG WORKSHEET

Returned ____ **Checked out** ____

Date of Presentation ______________________

To Whom ______________________

Telephone ______________________

Location ______________________ G / M / I / Other

Presentation In Person ____ By a Rep ____ By Mail ____

Other ______________________

Materials Used Standard Package ____

Other ______________________

Date Return Requested ______________________

Date Materials Returned ______________________

Returned ____ **Checked out** ____

Date of Presentation ______________________

To Whom ______________________

Telephone ______________________

Location ______________________ G / M / I / Other

Presentation In Person ____ By a Rep ____ By Mail ____

Other ______________________

Materials Used Standard Package ____

Other ______________________

Date Return Requested ______________________

Date Materials Returned ______________________

Returned ____ **Checked out** ____

Date of Presentation ______________________

To Whom ______________________

Telephone ______________________

Location ______________________ G / M / I / Other

Presentation In Person ____ By a Rep ____ By Mail ____

Other ______________________

Materials Used Standard Package ____

Other ______________________

Date Return Requested ______________________

Date Materials Returned ______________________

BILL OF SALE

Place

____
(Gallery, Museum, Art Show, Studio, or Business)

Sold to

____
(Name of Buyer)

____
(Address of Buyer)

____
(Phone Number of Buyer)

Sold by

____
(Name of Seller—Artist or Authorized Dealer)

____
(Address of Seller)

____
(Phone Number of Seller)

Description of Work

____
(Title)

____
(Subject, Media, Dimensions)

____
(Description)

Price

____
(Complete Purchase Price)

Terms of Payment

____

Reproduction Rights Reserved by the Artist

____
(Purchaser's Signature)

____
(Artist or Authorized Dealer's Signature)

Date

____

CERTIFICATE OF AUTHENTICITY—ORIGINAL ARTWORK

Certificate of Authenticity

Artist ______________________________

Title ______________________________

Media ______________________________

Dimensions ______________________________

Year ______________________________

Comments ____

This is to certify that the artwork described above and attached hereto is an original work by the named artist.

____

(Artist or Authorized Dealer's Signature) (Date)

CERTIFICATE OF AUTHENTICITY—ORIGINAL PRINT

Certificate of Authenticity

Artist ____________________

Title ____________________

Media ____________________

Dimensions ____________________

Publisher ____________________

Year ____________________

Number of authorized signed prints in this edition ______

Number of other editions ______

Number of artist proofs ______

Size of other editions ______

Number of unsigned proofs ______

Comments: ____________________

This is to certify that the artwork described above and attached hereto is an original print by the named artist.

____

(Artist or Authorized Dealer's Signature) (Date)

PROVENANCE

This document serves as first issue of Provenance

Type of Art ____________________

Artist ____________________

Title ____________________

Dimensions ____________________

Year ____________________

This artwork was completed by the artist in _______________ and was signed and so designated by the artist as to the year of completion and authenticity.

This artwork was acquired by ____________ in ______.
(Seller) (Year of Purchase)

Ownership of the above described work was transferred to:

____
(Name of Buyer)

____
(Address of Buyer)

____
(Phone Number of Buyer)

on _______ for the sum of: _______________________________.
(Sale Date) (Purchase Price)

As of this date, ownership of this painting remains with __________.

____
(Seller's Signature) (Date)

EXHIBITION AGREEMENT

This Exhibition Agreement is made and entered into to be effective as of the ____ day of ______ 19___, by and between _____________, sometimes referred to as "Artist," and ______________, sometimes referred to as "Authorized Representative," providing exhibition space for the works described hereto, sometimes referred to as "Space."

The purpose of this agreement is to set forth the understandings governing the agreed to exhibition by Artist of the described works of art in the Exhibition Space.

Artist

____
(Name of Artist)

____
(Address)

____
(Telephone)

Exhibition Space

____
(Name of Space)

____
(Location of Space)

____
(Authorized Representative for Space)

Artworks for Exhibition

Title	Media	Dimensions	Year

Duration _____________ to _____________
(Starting Date of Exhibition) (Ending Date of Exhibition)

____
(Exhibition Hours Open to the Public)

No works shall be removed from the Space's premises until sold or returned to the Artist, unless otherwise agreed upon in writing.

Installation Artist / Space (circle one) shall be solely responsible for the installation of the exhibition. Installation shall begin on ______ , 19 ___ and be completed by _____ , 19 __. All final installation decisions shall be the sole responsibility of the Space staff. Materials required for installation, including mountings, tape, pins, nails, and similar items as required are the responsibility of the Artist / Space *(circle one).*

Delivery Artworks are to arrive at the Space on _____ , 19 ___ by ___ am/pm. Artworks shall be confirmed as received by _______.

Shipment of the works to the Space shall be arranged by _______ and paid for by _____________ including insurance. Artist shall advise the Space in writing of the prices and insurance values for each work to be exhibited by _____ , 19 ___.

Insurance Space shall insure the works for the values assigned by the Artist from the period when the works arrive at the Space until the works are removed from the Space. The Space is responsible for security of all works while present on the Space premises. The Space represents that it is in sound repair and shall be responsible for damage to the works as a result of structural defects, water damage, vandalism, theft, or the like. The Space shall exercise reasonable care in dealing with the works.

The Space shall maintain all public and exhibition areas in a good state of repair, clean and orderly.

Promotions The following publicity and promotions shall be provided for this exhibition:

_____	Invitations	Artist / Space / Shared
_____	Press Releases	Artist / Space / Shared
_____	Public Service Announcements	Artist / Space / Shared
_____	Advertisements	Artist / Space / Shared
_____	Posters	Artist / Space / Shared
_____	Brochure/Catalog	Artist / Space / Shared
_____	Artists Reception	Artist / Space / Shared
_____	Other ________________	Artist / Space / Shared

The costs of promotions shall be reimbursed to the Artist and/or Space as agreed upon hereto:

Within seven days of the close of the exhibition the gallery will pay all monies owed to artist.

Deinstallation Artist / Space (circle one) shall be solely responsible for the deinstallation of the exhibition. Deinstallation shall begin on ____ , 19____ and be completed by _____, 19___.

Artworks not sold during the exhibition are to be returned to the artist by _____, 19 __ by ___ am/pm. Return shipment of the works will be arranged by _______ and paid for by _______ , including insurance based on the values provided at time of delivery.

Remuneration In remuneration for exhibiting and selling the Artist's works, the Space shall receive a _____ percent commission on the Net / Gross (circle one) sale of the art.

For commissions based on net sales values, the following expenses shall be subtracted from the sale revenues prior to determining the total commission to be paid the Space:

____

Artist is to receive the monies from the sale of the work within ____ days of receipt from the purchaser. Delinquency in payment will activate a ___ percent penalty to be subtracted from the Space's commission.

Amendments Amendments, modifications, supplements or changes to this Agreement shall be in writing and signed by both parties.

Termination of Agreement by Both Parties Either party may terminate this Agreement by giving to the other party sixty (60) days notice in writing.

Laws Governing Agreement This agreement shall be governed by and construed in accordance with the laws of the State of California.

Both parties agree that this represents the entire understanding between them, and that it shall be a binding contract upon the signature of the Artist and an authorized representative of the Space.

____

(Artist or Authorized Dealer's Signature) (Date)

____

(Authorized Space Representative) (Date)

CONSIGNMENT AGREEMENT

It is hereby agreed between ______________________, hereinafter referred to as "owner" of the artworks described in Schedule A, attached hereto, and _________________, hereinafter referred to as "dealer," that dealer shall exhibit and offer the described artwork for sale to dealer's clients under the following conditions:

1. The works hereby consigned to the dealer as agent for the owner and described herein are priced at net to owner on the attached list. All works shall remain the property of the owner unless and until they are purchased by collectors or the dealer.
2. The works shall be exhibited or made available for inspection by prospective purchasers by the dealer from _________, 19___ until this agreement is terminated by owner or dealer upon thirty (30) days' written notice to the other party.
3. The owner will assist the dealer by framing all works hereby consigned. The owner's incurred costs in framing will be returned to the owner in addition to the sale price of the work of art.
4. The dealer will pay the owner the net price hereby established and agreed upon per the attached inventory sheet on any works sold by the dealer. Notice of all sales will be given to the owner at the conclusion of each month and payment of all monies due shall be made not more than thirty days after the receipt of payment by the dealer. The dealer assumes full risk of nonpayment by the purchaser.
5. During the term of this agreement and during shipping from and to the owner, the dealer shall cause all of owner's work consigned to the dealer to be insured to the benefit of owner against any and all loss in an amount equal to the owner's net amount.
6. No unsold works shall be removed from the dealer's premises until the works are sold to a purchaser unless agreed upon in writing.
7. The owner shall have the right to inventory all consigned works at reasonable times and to obtain a full accounting for any works not present at the dealer's premises at such time.
8. The owner, as copyright owner of the hereby consigned works, reserves all rights to the reproduction of the works in any manner. This restriction shall be indicated by the dealer in writing on all sales invoices and memoranda. However, the owner will not withhold permission for the reproduction of such works for promotional purposes if all such reproductions are submitted to owner for approval prior to any printing and distribution of said promotional materials.

Page 1 of 3

9. This agreement shall at all times be governed by the laws of the state of _______________ .

____

(Artist's Signature) (Date)

____

(Artist's Printed Name)

____

(Artist's Street Address)

____

(Artist's City, State, ZIP, and Country Address)

____

(Artist's Telephone Number(s))

____

(Authorized Representative's Signature) (Date)

____

(Authorized Representative's Printed Name)

____

(Venue Name)

____

(Venue Street Address)

____

(Venue City, State, ZIP, and Country Address)

____

(Venue Telephone Number(s))

Schedule A

Total Number of Pieces Consigned under This Agreement: ____

____

(Title) (Year Created)

(Subject, Media, Dimensions)

(Description)

____

(Title) (Year Created)

(Subject, Media, Dimensions)

(Description)

____

(Title) (Year Created)

(Subject, Media, Dimensions)

(Description)

____

(Title) (Year Created)

(Subject, Media, Dimensions)

(Description)

Page 3 of 3

CONDITION REPORT

Name of Lender ______________________________

Name of Institution ______________________________

Address ______________________________

City, State, ZIP ______________________________

Artist ______________________________

Title ______________________________

Dimensions ______________________________

Media ______________________________

Year ______________________________

This report is to document the condition of the above described artwork at this time of receipt ________, 19___ by the institution.

Condition of frame ______________________________

Condition of paint, canvas, etc. indicating any minor blemishes ______________________________
____

Report any abnormal condition of the artwork ______________________________
____

Indicate by photo or diagram any and all suspicious or damaged areas. Attach said documentation to this report and lender's copy. Immediately notify lender of damage.

____

(Registrar's Signature) (Institution)

ARTWORK DOCUMENTATION FOR THE ARTIST

Type of Work ____________________

Category ____________________

Catalog Number ____________________

Artist ____________________

Title ____________________

Description ____________________

Size ____________________

Medium ____________________

Completion Date ____________________

Date Acquired by ____________________

Framed Yes _____ No _____

Exhibits

(Location)	**(Dates of Exhibition)**		
____________________	__________	to	__________
____________________	__________	to	__________
____________________	__________	to	__________

Scholarship Yes _____ No _____

Condition Report on File Yes _____ No _____

Estimated Value ____________________

Appraisal Value ____________________

Date Sold ____________________

Name of Buyer ____________________

Address ____________________

City, State, ZIP ____________________

Sales Price ____________________

INVITATION WORKSHEET

Your Name ______________________________

Event Name ______________________________

Event Dates ______________________________

Artist's Reception
(Day, Date, Time) ______________________________

Location Name ______________________________

Location Address ______________________________

Contact Phone ______________________________

Daily Hours ______________________________

Image Title ______________________________

PRESS RELEASE WORKSHEET

Venue Name ______________________

PRESS RELEASE

For additional information, contact:

Contact Name ______________________

Contact Phone Number ______________________

Artist's Last Name or Exhibition Name ______________________

City, State Location ______________________

Brief Statement about Event

____

____

____

____

Event Dates ______________________

Reception Day, Date, Time ______________________

Brief Artist Statement

____

____

____

____

____

____

Venue Name Repeated ______________________

Complete Venue Address ______________________

Venue Hours ______________________

PROMOTIONAL SCHEDULE

Once you have an exhibition, use this form to stay abreast of promotional considerations.

Four Months Prior to Exhibition

_____ Confirm exhibition details (participants, dates, opening reception, location, etc.).

_____ Design and print press releases.

_____ Submit press releases to magazines (longer deadline publications).

Three Months Prior to Exhibition

_____ Design and be prepared to print invitations.

_____ Design catalogs, brochures, and other print materials for the exhibition.

Two Months Prior to Exhibition

_____ Design and print posters (optional).

One Month Prior to Exhibition

_____ Print invitations.

_____ Print catalog, brochure, and other materials.

_____ Begin soliciting editorial review for your exhibition (dealer involvement).

_____ Plan details of the opening event (catering, music, VIP arrangements, etc.).

Two Weeks Prior to Exhibition

_____ Deliver public service announcements to radio and television stations.

_____ Mail invitations.

_____ Mail press releases to newspapers, art writers, and art critics (with and without photographs).

_____ Begin follow-up calls. (You will increase your attendance ten-fold with personal contact.)

_____ Arrange for a photographer (professional or amateur) to be present at opening.

One Week Prior to Exhibition

_____ Continue follow-up calls.

Day of Exhibition

_____ Attend the artist's reception.

Follow-Up (Within Two Weeks of Exhibition Closing)

_____ Send thank-you notes to key patrons of event.

_____ Update your mailing list with new people and corrected information.

_____ Follow up personally with those who expressed interest in purchasing your work. (Dealer should be involved.)

_____ Invite interested people to your gallery or studio.

PROMOTION CHECKLIST

To obtain the most from your promotional dollar, it is important to have a plan. Use this worksheet to select the types of promotions you wish to use in your plan. The options are divided into short- and long-term. Select those activities you will begin to use immediately and those you will pursue in the future.

		Today	1 Year	2 Years	Not in Plan
Short-term Promotional Options					
____	Invitations	____	____	____	____
____	Catalogs	____	____	____	____
____	Brochures	____	____	____	____
____	Tear Sheets	____	____	____	____
____	Press Releases—Newspapers	____	____	____	____
____	Press Releases—Magazines	____	____	____	____
____	Public Service Announcements—Television	____	____	____	____
____	Public Service Announcements—Radio	____	____	____	____
____	Editorials/Reviews	____	____	____	____
____	Posters	____	____	____	____
Special Events					
____	Charity Events	____	____	____	____
____	Open Houses at Your Studio	____	____	____	____
____	Demonstrations—Art Fairs/ Public Places	____	____	____	____
____	Lectures—Colleges/ Universities	____	____	____	____
Long-term Promotional Options					
____	Catalogs	____	____	____	____
____	Newsletters	____	____	____	____
____	Videos	____	____	____	____
____	Advertising	____	____	____	____
____	Articles for Publication	____	____	____	____
____	Guest Appearance—Television Shows	____	____	____	____
____	Guest Appearance—Radio Shows	____	____	____	____
____	Books on Your Art	____	____	____	____

Other Promotional Ideas

PRICE SCHEDULE STRUCTURES

Edition Size

Number of Prints Sold	**Wholesale**	**Retail**
1 to 25 prints	________	________
26 to 50 prints	________	________
51 to 75 prints	________	________
76 to 100 prints	________	________

Artist's proof: You can print 10 percent of your edition as artist's proofs.

Create a four-tier schedule based upon each tier being 25 percent of the entire edition. Include the cost of printing, promotion, shipping, and any other related expenses.

Cost per Unit to Produce ____________________

Total Cost of Production ____________________

Edition size ____________________

Tier 1

Prints ____________________

Wholesale ____________________

Suggested Retail ____________________

Tier 2

Prints ____________________

Wholesale ____________________

Suggested Retail ____________________

Tier 3

Prints ____________________

Wholesale ____________________

Suggested Retail ____________________

Tier 4

Prints ____________________

Wholesale ____________________

Suggested Retail ____________________

Net Profit earned from Wholesale Sales ____________________

Net Profit Earned from Direct Sales ____________________

Total Projected Production and Marketing Costs ____________________

Projected Total Net Profits: ____________________

PUBLISHING AGREEMENT

This is an agreement between ______________ (Artist) and ______________________, (A ____________________ Corporation).

The company will assume all costs for the publishing and distribution of all Artist's fine art reproductions, including sales and promotion. The Artist shall submit Artist's original art ______________________________ (paintings, sculpture, other) and the Company shall select which one(s) the Company will reproduce and distribute. Artist will not permit anyone else to reproduce any of Artist's original art during the period of this agreement.

The Company has the right to sell and promote Artist's reproductions through its network of dealers and in any other way it deems appropriate. Artist will, however, be consulted before decisions are made regarding sale, promotion, image size, and edition size whenever feasible.

The Company and Artist agree to keep confidential the terms of this Agreement, information related to the performance thereof, the business practices and marketing strategies, as well as concepts. This obligation shall survive the terms of this agreement.

The Company agrees to pay the Artist ten (10) percent of the gross sales of each reproduction. Payment will be made each month based upon the gross sales for the prior month. Artist will receive, at no charge, twenty-five artist's proofs of each original reproduced.

This agreement will remain in effect for ____________ years from the date of the official release of the first reproduction. If no written notice is given by either party ________ days prior to the end of the fifth year, the agreement will automatically be renewed by an additional ___________ years.

This agreement, together with all its benefits and obligations, shall be assignable by the Company, but Artist's services are unique and special and are not assignable.

This agreement constitutes the entire agreement between Artist and the Company and no verbal terms, other than as set forth herein, will be considered a part of the agreement between the parties.

Company:

____

Signature   Date

Artist/Client:

____

Signature   Date

PRESENTATION SCHEDULE

First Week or Monthly Presentations

Venue	Contact	Address	Phone

Second Week

Venue	Contact	Response

Third Week

Venue	Contact	Response

Fourth Week

Venue	Contact	Response

SALES RECORD

Title of Piece ____________________

Venue Type ____________
Time Listed ____________

Sold By ____________________
Contact Name ____________________
Address ____________________
City, State, ZIP ____________________
Telephone ____________________
Facsimile ____________________

Collector Type ____________

Sold To ____________________
Address ____________________
City, State, ZIP ____________________
Telephone ____________________
Facsimile ____________________

Sold for ____________
Monies
paid venue ____________

Listed Price ____________________
Net Monies
Received ____________________
Date of sale ________________________

Title of Piece ____________________

Date of sale ____________

Sold By ____________________
Contact Name ____________________
Address ____________________
City, State, ZIP ____________________
Telephone ____________________
Facsimile ____________________

Venue Type ____________
Time Listed ____________

Sold To ____________________
Address ____________________
City, State, ZIP ____________________
Telephone ____________________
Facsimile ____________________

Collector Type ____________

Listed Price ____________________
Net Monies
Received ____________________

Sold for ____________
Monies
paid venue ____________

TELEPHONE RESEARCH WORKSHEET: FUNDING OPPORTUNITIES

Date of Contact ____________________

Source of Listing ____________________

Referred by ____________________

Name of Funding ____________________

Name of Sponsoring Organization ____________________

Address ____________________

City, State, ZIP ____________________

Country ____________________

Telephone ____________________

Facsimile ____________________

Owner/Director ____________________

Title ____________________

Spoke with ____________________

Department ____________________

Date Funding Application is Due ____________________

Type of Funding?

____ Grant

____ Artist-in-Residency

____ Sponsorship

____ Other ____________________

Funding Criteria?

____

Do you meet all the required criteria? Yes ____ No ____

If "No," should you still pursue applying for this award? Yes ____ No ____

Maximum Award Amount ____________________

What other items are awarded? (housing, studio, exhibition space, teaching, etc.)

____

What are the terms of the award?

____

____

What materials are requested to be presented and how?

____

____

What is the purpose of the award?

____

____

What is the focus of the sponsoring organization?

____

____

What are your feelings about the organization's focus, beliefs, products, and activities?

____

____

Name the artists who have received funding in prior years.

____

____

You may wish to call the artists who have been awarded a grant in prior years to ask questions about the organization, application process, their presentation, and other aspects of the grant.

Comments

____

____

APPLICATION TRACKING WORKSHEET

Name of Funder ______________________

Name of Sponsoring Organization ______________________

Telephone ______________________

Application Due ______________________

Application Submitted ______________________

Confirmation of Receipt ______________________

First Review Cut ______________________

Second Review Cut ______________________

Third Review Cut ______________________

Fourth Review Cut ______________________

Final Decision ______________________

Appointment for Presentation ______________________

Appointment for Interview ______________________

Final Outcome ______________________

____

____

Notes and images from application (Remember to retain a copy of the completed application for your records):

____

____

____

WRITER'S QUESTIONNAIRE FOR THE ARTIST

Treat each question as an interview from which your writer will get to know more about you and your art and in turn may select quotes to include in your essay. If you have any additional statements beyond the topics discussed below, feel free to include them.

Remember to provide slides and/or photographs of your works for the writer to view. Ideally, if you have selected the images that are to be used in your catalog, provide slides of those works, properly labeled with your name, the title of the image, media, dimensions, and year of creation. Indicate which image you have selected for the cover.

Date ______________________________

Artist Name ______________________________

Telephone ______________________________

Fax ______________________________

Internet ______________________________

1. Are you a symbolic artist? Yes ___ No ___

2. Where do you derive your symbols from?

____

____

____

3. Who is your art for?

____

____

____

4. What is more important, the moment and act of creation, the message, or the material artwork?

____

____

____

5. If you could not earn money through art, would you still be an artist?

6. What is the role of the viewer relative to your artwork?

7. What is the role of spontaneity and of control in your artwork?

8. Discuss the elements of your artistic language.

9. What event most influenced your work and your choice to be an artist?

10. What artists have had the greatest influence on your work?

11. Is there a single, proper interpretation of your artwork?

____

____

____

12. Under what conditions would you refuse to sell or to have your works displayed?

____

____

____

13. What is unique about your work?

____

____

____

14. Is there a particular name you have for your style of art?

____

____

____

15. What is art, and how has it changed your life?

____

____

____

16. Is your art more personal, social, political, or nonobjective?

____

____

____

17. What is the role of emotion in the creation, the understanding, and the experience of your art?

____

____

____

18. Is your art representational?

Yes _____ No _____ In what sense?

____

____

____

19. Is your art abstract?

Yes _____ No _____ In what sense?

____

____

____

20. What are the unexplored frontiers for your art?

____

____

____

21. How important are the general public and the artistic community to your work?

____

____

____

22. How would you like for history to remember your art?

____

____

____

23. Is there a medium you wish to explore?

____

____

____

24. Why do you work in the medium that you do?

____

____

____

CATALOG MOCKUP

PAGE 1—COVER

A. Position your name and image on the page to suit your design.

B. For perfect bound catalogs, use your name at the top and the name of the institution at the bottom. If your catalog does not have a connection with an exhibition, use your name only centered in the middle of the bound edge of the catalog.

C. If your catalog is bound by staples or stitched, you may wish to move "B" 1/4" to the right of "C" (this is optional).

PAGE 2

Position the title of the cover piece on the bottom.

EXAMPLE:

1.
WHITE DOG
Oil on canvas
19" × 30"
1997

PAGE 3

Position the title in the center of the page.

EXAMPLE:

Title of Exhibition
Name of the Artist
Medium
Date

Lorem ipsum dolor sit amet, consectetuer adipiscing elit, sed diam nonummy nibh euismod tincidunt ut laoreet dolore magna aliquam erat volutpat. Ut wisi enim ad minim veniam, quis nostrud exerci tation ullamcorper suscipit lobortis nisl ut aliquip ex ea commodo consequat. Duis autem vel eum iriure dolor in hendrerit in vulputate velit esse molestie consequat, vel illum dolore eu feugiat nulla facilisis at vero eros et accumsan et iusto odio dignissim qui blandit praesent luptatum zzril delenit augue duis dolore te feugait nulla facilisi. Lorem ipsum dolor sit amet, consectetuer adipiscing elit, sed diam nonummy nibh euismod tincidunt ut laoreet dolore magna aliquam erat volutpat. Ut wisi enim ad minim veniam, quis nostrud exerci tation ullamcorper suscipit lobortis nisl ut aliquip ex ea commodo consequat.

Duis autem vel eum iriure dolor in hendrerit in vulputate velit esse molestie consequat, vel illum dolore eu feugiat nulla facilisis at vero eros et accumsan et iusto odio dignissim qui blandit praesent luptatum zzril delenit augue duis dolore te feugait nulla facilisi. Nam liber tempor cum soluta nobis eleifend option congue nihil imperdiet doming id quod mazim placerat facer possim assum. Lorem ipsum dolor sit amet, consectetuer adipiscing elit, sed diam nonummy nibh euismod tincidunt ut laoreet dolore magna aliquam erat volutpat. Ut wisi enim ad minim veniam, quis nostrud exerci tation ullamcorper suscipit lobortis nisl ut aliquip ex ea commodo consequat. Duis autem vel eum iriure dolor in hendrerit in vulputate velit esse molestie consequat, vel illum dolore eu feugiat nulla facilisis at vero eros et accumsan et iusto odio dignissim qui blandit praesent luptatum zzril delenit augue duis dolore te feugait nulla facilisi. Lorem ipsum dolor sit amet, consectetuer adipiscing elit, sed diam nonummy nibh euismod tincidunt ut laoreet dolore magna aliquam erat volutpat.

PAGE 4—ESSAY

Position text on page to balance each side.

Lorem ipsum dolor sit amet, consectetuer adipiscing elit, sed diam nonummy nibh euismod tincidunt ut laoreet dolore magna aliquam erat volutpat. Ut wisi enim ad minim veniam, quis nostrud exerci tation ullamcorper suscipit lobortis nisl ut aliquip ex ea commodo consequat. Duis autem vel eum iriure dolor in hendrerit in vulputate velit esse molestie consequat, vel illum dolore eu feugiat nulla facilisis at vero eros et accumsan et iusto odio dignissim qui blandit praesent luptatum zzril delenit augue duis dolore te feugait nulla facilisi. Lorem ipsum dolor sit amet, consectetuer adipiscing elit, sed diam nonummy nibh euismod tincidunt ut laoreet dolore magna aliquam erat volutpat. Ut wisi enim ad minim veniam, quis nostrud exerci tation ullamcorper suscipit lobortis nisl ut aliquip ex ea commodo consequat.

Duis autem vel eum iriure dolor in hendrerit in vulputate velit esse molestie consequat, vel illum dolore eu feugiat nulla facilisis at vero eros et accumsan et iusto odio dignissim qui blandit praesent luptatum zzril delenit augue duis dolore te feugait nulla facilisi. Nam liber tempor cum soluta nobis eleifend option congue nihil imperdiet doming id quod mazim placerat facer possim assum. Lorem ipsum dolor sit amet, consectetuer adipiscing elit, sed diam nonummy nibh euismod tincidunt ut laoreet dolore magna aliquam erat volutpat. Ut wisi enim ad minim veniam, quis nostrud exerci tation ullamcorper suscipit lobortis nisl ut aliquip ex ea commodo consequat. Duis autem vel eum iriure dolor in hendrerit in vulputate velit esse molestie consequat, vel illum dolore eu feugiat nulla facilisis at vero eros et accumsan et iusto odio dignissim qui blandit praesent luptatum zzril delenit augue duis dolore te feugait nulla facilisi. Lorem ipsum dolor sit amet, consectetuer adipiscing elit, sed diam nonummy nibh euismod tincidunt ut laoreet dolore magna aliquam erat volutpat.

Author's name

PAGE 5—ESSAY

Position text on page to balance each side.

______

Title ______________________________

Media ______________________________

Size ______________________________

Year ______________________________

PAGE 6

EXAMPLE:

2.
RED DOG
Oil on canvas
19" × 30"
1997

PAGE 7

Position your image to suit your presentation design. Be sure to balance the image with the text.

Title ______________

Media ______________

Size ______________

Year ______________

PAGE 8

EXAMPLE:

3.
BLACK DOG
Oil on canvas
19" × 30"
1997

PAGE 9

Position your image to suit your presentation design. Be sure to balance the image with the text.

______

Title ______________________________

Media ______________________________

Size ______________________________

Year ______________________________

PAGE 10

EXAMPLE:

4.
BLUE DOG
Oil on canvas
19" × 30"
1997

PAGE 11

Position your image to suit your presentation design. Be sure to balance the image with the text.

______

Title ______________________________

Media ______________________________

Size ______________________________

Year ______________________________

PAGE 12

EXAMPLE:

5.
PINK DOG
Oil on canvas
19" × 30"
1997

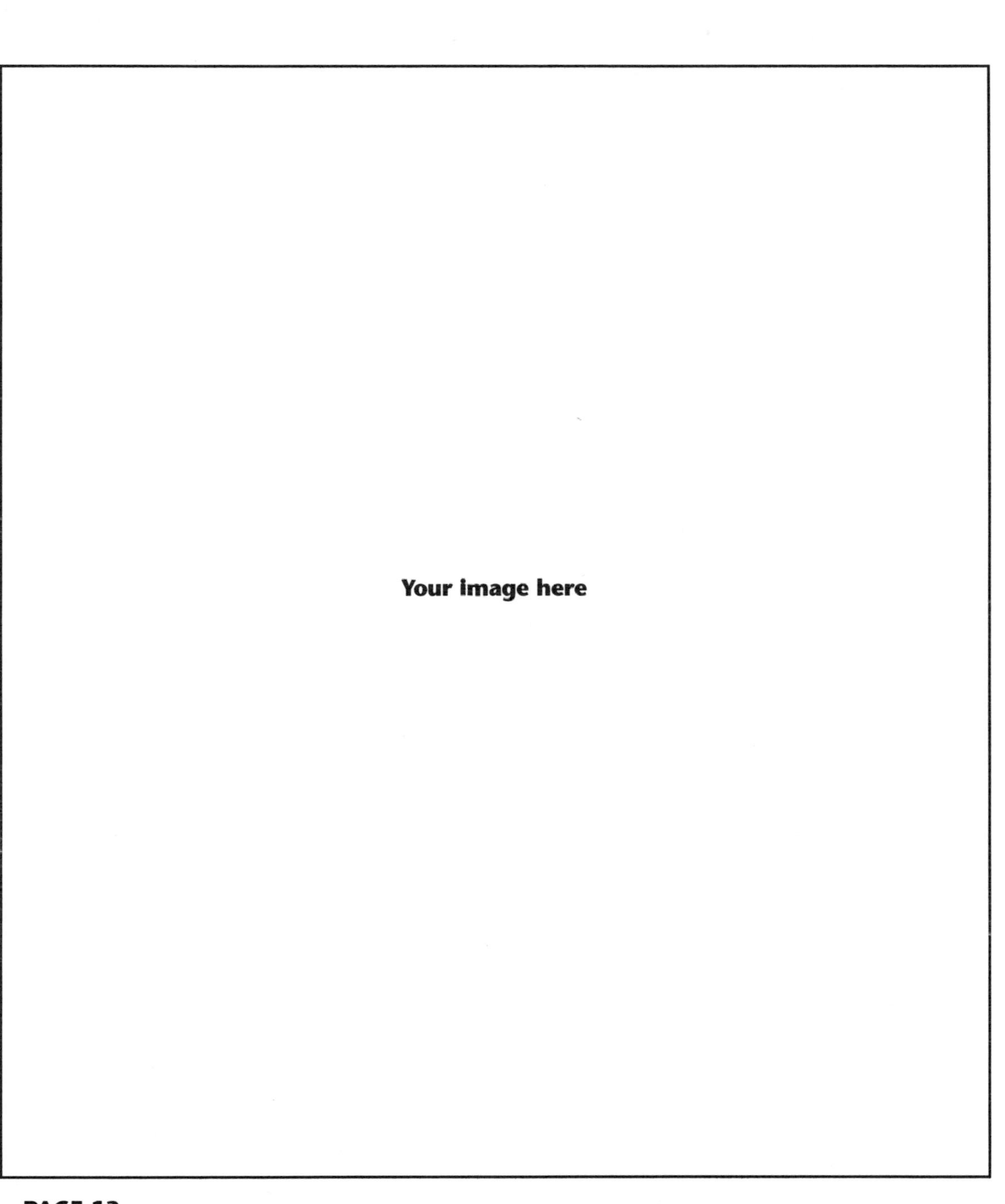

PAGE 13

Position your image to suit your presentation design. Be sure to balance the image with the text.

Title ______________________

Media ______________________

Size ______________________

Year ______________________

PAGE 14

EXAMPLE:

6.
YELLOW DOG
Oil on canvas
19" × 30"
1997

PAGE 15

Position your image to suit your presentation design. Be sure to balance the image with the text.

Title ________________

Media ________________

Size ________________

Year ________________

PAGE 16

EXAMPLE:

7.
GREEN DOG
Oil on canvas
19" × 30"
1997

PAGE 17

Position your image to suit your presentation design. Be sure to balance the image with the text.

Title ______________________

Media ______________________

Size ______________________

Year ______________________

PAGE 18

EXAMPLE:

8.
MAUVE DOG
Oil on canvas
19" × 30"
1997

PAGE 19

Position your image to suit your presentation design. Be sure to balance the image with the text.

Title ______________________

Media ______________________

Size ______________________

Year ______________________

PAGE 20

EXAMPLE:

9.
UNTITLED
Oil on canvas
19" × 30"
1997

PAGE 21

Position your image to suit your presentation design. Be sure to balance the image with the text.

A. Lorem ipsum dolor sit amet, consectetuer adipiscing elit, sed diam nonummy nibh euismod tincidunt ut laoreet dolore magna aliquam erat volutpat. Ut wisi enim ad minim veniam, quis nostrud exerci tation ullamcorper suscipit lobortis nisl ut aliquip ex ea commodo consequat. Duis autem vel eum iriure dolor in hendrerit in vulputate velit esse molestie consequat, vel illum dolore eu feugiat nulla facilisis at vero eros et accumsan et iusto odio dignissim qui blandit praesent luptatum zzril delenit augue duis dolore te feugait nulla facilisi. Lorem ipsum dolor sit amet, consectetuer adipiscing elit, sed diam nonummy nibh euismod tincidunt ut laoreet dolore magna aliquam erat volutpat. Ut wisi enim ad minim veniam, quis nostrud exerci tation ullamcorper suscipit lobortis nisl ut aliquip ex ea commodo consequat.

B. Duis autem vel eum iriure dolor in hendrerit in vulputate velit esse molestie consequat, vel illum dolore eu feugiat nulla facilisis at vero eros et accumsan et iusto odio dignissim qui blandit praesent luptatum zzril delenit augue duis dolore te feugait nulla facilisi. Nam liber tempor cum soluta nobis eleifend option congue nihil imperdiet doming id quod mazim placerat facer possim assum. Lorem ipsum dolor sit amet, consectetuer adipiscing elit, sed diam nonummy nibh euismod tincidunt ut laoreet dolore magna aliquam erat volutpat. Ut wisi enim ad minim veniam, quis nostrud exerci tation ullamcorper suscipit lobortis nisl ut aliquip ex ea commodo consequat. Duis autem vel eum iriure dolor in hendrerit in vulputate velit esse molestie consequat, vel illum dolore eu feugiat nulla facilisis at vero eros et accumsan et iusto odio dignissim qui blandit praesent luptatum zzril delenit augue duis dolore te feugait nulla facilisi. Lorem ipsum dolor sit amet, consectetuer adipiscing elit, sed diam nonummy nibh euismod tincidunt ut laoreet dolore magna aliquam erat volutpat.

PAGE 22

A. Artist's Statement

B. Biographical Information

PAGE 23—CREDIT INFORMATION PAGE

Position the credit information in the lower inside of the page.

EXAMPLE:

Title of Exhibition
Essay: Author of Essay
Organization
Catalog Design

PAGE 24-BACK COVER